Camelot, Inc.

CAMELOT, INC.

LEADERSHIP AND MANAGEMENT INSIGHTS FROM KING ARTHUR AND THE ROUND TABLE

Paul Oestreicher

 PRAEGER

AN IMPRINT OF ABC-CLIO, LLC
Santa Barbara, California • Denver, Colorado • Oxford, England

Library of Congress Cataloging-in-Publication Data

Oestreicher, Paul.
   Camelot, Inc. : leadership and management insights from King Arthur and the Round Table / Paul Oestreicher.
      p. cm.
   Includes bibliographical references and index.
   ISBN 978-0-313-38695-4 (alk. paper)—ISBN 978-0-313-38696-1 (ebook)
1. Leadership. 2. Management. 3. Arthurian romances. [1. Arthur, King—Legends.] I. Title.
   HD57.7.O364   2011
   658.4'092—dc22   2010045111

ISBN: 978-0-313-38695-4
EISBN: 978-0-313-38696-1

15   14   13   12   11   1   2   3   4   5

This book is also available on the World Wide Web as an eBook.
Visit www.abc-clio.com for details.

Praeger
An Imprint of ABC-CLIO, LLC

ABC-CLIO, LLC
130 Cremona Drive, P.O. Box 1911
Santa Barbara, California 93116-1911

This book is printed on acid-free paper ∞

Manufactured in the United States of America

For Deborah
and
Robin, Laura, Jessica, and Rebecca

CONTENTS

PREFACE

My wife, Deborah, was the one who gave me a nudge to read *The Once and Future King* early in our relationship. We discussed favorite books and found, to no big surprise, that we had many in common. As I started to read the books on her list that I had missed in my youth, I came upon T. H. White's classic; it was one of those books I had always promised myself that I'd get to at some point down the road. Finding that she owned not one but two copies, I knew that consuming this book had to be a priority.

Like White, who read Sir Thomas Malory's epic *Le Morte d'Arthur*, penned in the 15th century, and saw relevance to 20th-century wartime Europe, I had an "aha" moment of my own from White's retelling of the Arthur stories. Arthur and his court sometimes planned and sometimes bumbled, sometimes succeeded and sometimes failed, in ways very similar to what we see today in modern organizations and institutions. Examining White's book, as well as other writings, we can take away crucial lessons in both leadership and management: the issues involving people and the issues involving process.

We know that people and their problems are mixtures of characteristics and circumstances. They need to be taken together as a package. Therefore, this book will cover a landscape of subjects instead of plumbing the depths of just a few so that we can gain a broad perspective on the range of challenges that confront us, learn to recognize them, and find a way forward.

ACKNOWLEDGMENTS

This book started as a hobby project. Exploring the stories of Arthur and Camelot was of personal interest and had the benefit of keeping me occupied during my commutes on the train. When I got it in my head that this recreational pursuit could grow into a book, I shared some early chapters with my friend and NYU colleague John Doorley. His support and encouragement propelled me to search for a publisher.

Discussions with Helio Fred Garcia, another valued NYU colleague, helped me to gain some new perspectives on the subjects of strategic communication and reputation management.

I owe a debt to the late Peter Drucker, whose books set the standard in explaining leadership and management principles and may never be equaled.

Andy Gilman of the CommCore Consulting Group introduced me to the world of messaging and positioning when I made the transition from research and development to communications and public affairs.

Important lessons on trust, teamwork, and team communication came from working years ago with Bob Kornecki, one of the finest public relations executives I've known.

Bob Ivry, cousin, friend, and reporter extraordinaire at Bloomberg, provided crucial critiques to the book manuscript and sharpened some otherwise blurry language.

Helping me to navigate through the world of publishing were Jeff Olson and his successor at Praeger Publishers, Brian Romer.

Annette Oestreicher Grollman, my loving aunt, inspired me early on with her excellence in science and writing.

Finally, my wonderful wife Deborah, and our daughters, Robin, Laura, Jessica, and Rebecca, were understanding beyond measure during the long process of researching and writing this book.

To all, you have my deep appreciation and thanks.

INTRODUCTION: THE RELEVANCE OF CAMELOT TO TODAY'S LEADERS AND INSTITUTIONS

Do you think that they, with their Battles, Famine, Black Death and Serfdom, were less enlightened than we are, with our Wars, Blockade, Influenza and Conscription?

If it takes a million years for a fish to become a reptile, has Man, in our few hundred, altered out of recognition?[1]

What lessons about management and leadership can an ancient king and court bring to us in the 21st century? Can the trials and tribulations of people so removed from us in time and custom truly be relevant in modern corporations, organizations, or governments? Have our problems and issues grown too complex for any pertinent comparisons? Have our customs and cultures evolved too far as to be unrecognizable to the past?

If one thinks of texts and stories even more ancient than those of King Arthur, the answer is obvious. People continue to draw important meaning from the stone tablets, scrolls, and books of the past. Indeed, there are many for whom ancient ways and teachings enhance their well-being and guide their daily lives. The Roman emperor and philosopher Marcus Aurelius wrote (before the time of Arthur, in the second century), "If you have seen the present then you have seen everything—as it has been since the beginning, as it will be forever." It was in the 19th century that the French journalist Jean-Baptiste Alphonse Karr wrote his famous epigram, "The more things change, the more they stay the same (*Plus ça change, plus c'est la même chose*)." And Winston Churchill remarked, "The further backward you look, the further forward you can see."

So it is with the stories of King Arthur. Life's lessons during the time of Camelot and the Round Table remain relevant because, at the core, they are about the human relationships that connect us, divide us, and drive us forward (or backward) in our various dealings—personal, business, or otherwise. Looking at the past, we can gain the accumulated wisdom from so many people, conflicts, and circumstances. Those enduring qualities and complexities of human nature, told and retold in story, song, and scripture, have given us guidance and assurance in the past and will continue to do so in the future. Thus, making workplace decisions or adopting a management philosophy based on the experiences of a current lifestyle guru or celebrity CEO might be riskier than thinking back to what history or legend can reveal.

You'll see that among Arthur's great initiatives was the attempt to embed the philosophy of Equal Justice into his warring society. This bold but necessary undertaking sought to create a new civilization based on fairness, compassion, and unity. To the cynical, it may sound a bit utopian and, possibly, politically expedient. But these are the underpinnings of good and sound institutions. This was a new and better way of valuing individuals, settling disputes, and solving problems.

Unfortunately for Arthur and his followers, there was still too much distrust, greed, and close-mindedness to allow Equal Justice to become fully entrenched in their world. Today, of course, we still encounter these barriers and diversions, but we're fortunate that the baseline of accountability and ethical behavior has moved forward.

As one looks back through human history, though, it's clear that our nature has not changed nearly as much as our surroundings. The power bases from which our leaders draw their authority have changed from the throne and the houses of worship to the boardroom and government capitals. But although the places may have morphed significantly in the last few millennia, our brains have not. Our grey matter would be indistinguishable from that of our medieval ancestors. Yet, our minds do change. Regarding which style of leadership is most desirable or most in fashion, we've seen the pendulum swing back and forth from kings to anonymous managers and then back to the kings—the kings of the boardroom, the celebrity CEOs. The leadership pendulum continues to swing but now at a different angle, impelled by the public markets and an exploding number of media channels. In the wake of the economic bubbles of the 2000s, the charismatic, media-hungry CEO lost ground to the pragmatic, media-savvy CEO.

Our elected officials, too, have found ways to amplify their power and extend their tenures by creating their own aura through the use of message testing and media relations. Getting elected in the United States means operating a large, cash-hungry organization. Thus, politicians have become productized; they are each a "brand" that they hope will resonate with their local constituents or to an even broader base if they have higher ambitions.

Whereas politicians have found success by tapping into our pop culture trends and "reality"-based media, Arthur had to invent a new cultural norm with very limited means of communication. There was no information superhighway or electronic media of any sort, of course; even the daily newspaper was centuries off. He had to use word-of-mouth and person-to-person contact to implement his experiment of developing new societal norms built around a code of justice.

Arthur tried to control what was controllable. Unfortunately, a weak communications infrastructure was a substantial obstacle. For a plan as grand as changing a national mindset, the delivery, acceptance, and implementation depend on a rapid and accurate two-way flow of information. Indeed, this is important for any idea or for life's everyday business. We have the same problem today.

Even with the inevitable barriers and impediments, we usually have options. Sometimes we choose well and other times we do not. The decision makers during the time of Camelot show that there are as many lessons on what to do as there are on what not to do. Like us all, the characters in old England did not always make the best decisions or use their insight to the greatest advantage. At various times, they displayed weaknesses of character and faith. Some were simple in their naïveté, and some were simply corrupt. Many times, intentions were pure but results were fouled by the intervention of others or a lack of resolve. The terrible grief, hard victories, and inglorious defeats that Arthur and his followers experienced sound contrary to the idealized picture of Camelot that Broadway, Hollywood, and Washington have, for the most part, painted for us.

No one can have it all or choose the correct path every time—not the nobles, the king, or his trusted inner circle. Yet we can trust our instincts, learn from others, influence what we are able to sway, stay the course when the plan seems right, and be willing to take risks and move in other directions when the planned results don't materialize within a predetermined timeframe.

In this book, we will glean management and leadership insights from Arthur's evolution from the awkward and out-of-place squire derisively called the Wart to impatient student to compassionate king to tired ruler. We'll start at a time when Arthur found a mentor (rather, when the mentor found him) and observe how he learned, how he developed his leadership philosophy and his vehicle for communications, what it took to excel, how he created a vision and mission, and then how a failure to confront issues led to his decline.

It's not just that these royal life-cycle transitions so closely track the rise and fall of modern managers and leaders. Arthur will help us to deal with some of today's most pressing leadership issues: knowledge retention, developing coherent plans and proposals, building internal and external advocacy, communicating and negotiating, team building, maintaining ethical standards, innovating, ensuring flexibility, moving from vision to execution, and succession planning.

Much of what we hear and what we come to accept as fact or truth has been termed "conventional wisdom." Here, we have Camelot wisdom. This will not be a history lesson, but I will use history to illustrate the dos and don'ts critical to our success as learners and leaders.

Before We Begin:
A Quick Review of
Arthur's Life

King Arthur is said to have lived in the sixth century, although scholars disagree on a precise time or even if he existed at all. There was mention of Arthur in *Historia Brittonum* (*The History of the Britons*), written in the ninth century, but he became firmly entrenched in the literary record following the publication of the popular *History of the Kings of Britain* by Geoffrey of Monmouth in the 12th century.

There are many accounts of King Arthur, but the version of events as written by T. H. White is perhaps the most beloved and the one upon which most of us (whether we knew it or not) base our vision of Arthur, Guinevere, Lancelot, and all the characters, places, and objects we associate with Camelot. After all, White's *The Once and Future King*, a 20th-century retelling of Sir Thomas Malory's 15th-century *Le Morte d'Arthur* (*The Death of Arthur*), was the original basis for Broadway's (1960) and Hollywood's (1967) Lerner and Loewe musical *Camelot* and Disney's animated classic *The Sword in the Stone*, released in 1963. (Malory, in turn, used the early 13th century's *Vulgate Cycle* and *Post-Vulgate Cycle* as starting material for his own work.)

The first glimpse we get of Arthur in White's book is as a boy growing up in the household of Sir Ector, his foster father. Ector's biological son, Kay, usually treated Arthur as a brother, including a good deal of sibling rivalry, but it was clear that only the "real" son would become a knight. Arthur, who carried the unfortunate nickname of the Wart (because it was a play on Art and not for any dermatologic reason), was destined to be Kay's squire, a knight's attendant.

Merlin, the sorcerer, met Arthur and became his mentor. Merlin was a powerful but, at times, mixed-up figure; he was living backward in time and occasionally found it difficult to distinguish between what was and what will be. Merlin focused his attention on Arthur and taught the future king about war, empathy, adaptation, and fairness by changing the Wart into a variety of creatures so that he could experience life through their eyes (or, in an episode when he was turned into an ant, antennae).

Approaching manhood, Kay was to be knighted and Arthur was to begin life as his squire when we are informed that the king of England, Uther Pendragon, died without an heir. Or did he? Arthur, we learn later, was the son of Pendragon by Igraine, the wife of Gorlois, the Earl of Cornwall. Pendragon, used some magical assistance from Merlin (yes, the same aforementioned preternatural mentor) to disguise himself and, deceived her into sleeping with him. In return for satisfying Pendragon's lust, Arthur was promised to Merlin.

Word spread throughout the land that an enchanted sword appeared in a church square in London. The sword's blade pierced through a smith's anvil and was, in turn, encased in a large rock beneath. On the pommel of the sword was inscribed, "Whoso Pulleth Out This Sword on This Stone and Anvil, Is Rightwise King Born of All England."

Sir Ector and his entourage, along with many other fortune seekers, traveled to London for a tournament to determine which brave knight would have the opportunity to pull the sword from the stone. Kay forgot to bring his sword to the match and commanded Arthur to retrieve his weapon. Finding no way to recover the sword from the locked inn where they were staying, Arthur came across the sword in the stone and drew it out with the help of the lessons he learned from the creatures of the forest. And thus his future was sealed.

As the new king, Arthur was confronted by a variety of enemies, including King Lot, the husband of the sociopathic and hateful Morgause. Lot's sons, Agravaine, Gaheris, Gareth, and Gawaine, had innate decency but were raised by the twisted Morgause to hate anyone outside their clan, especially Arthur. Morgause, Arthur's half-sister (a truth hidden from him at the time), tricked him into conceiving another child with her, Mordred. Hearing a prophecy that Mordred would one day cause his downfall, the young, unworldly king attempted to cast his son out of the kingdom, knowing that such an action could cause the baby's death. Not knowing his son's whereabouts, Arthur's order was implemented broadly and put other babies born at the same time in jeopardy. This collection of "sinful acts" plays prominently in Arthur's eventual downfall at the end of the tale.

Arthur inherited a kingdom steeped in brutality and rife with infighting among the nobles. He formulated a plan, blessed by Merlin, to stamp out the iniquities imposed on the population by redirecting force in the cause of justice: might for right. The king formed the Knights of the Round

Table to spread the word and help change the very culture of England. Arthur suppressed his enemies by defeating Lot's army at the momentous battle of Bedegraine, with the help of Kings Bors and Ban of France and by employing some radical battle tactics.

A key figure in winning battles, and hearts and minds, on behalf of Arthur was Sir Lancelot. Through years of toil and practice, Lancelot became the best knight in the world. Yet, Lancelot had significant failings. He was Arthur's best friend and top commander, but he was also the lover of the king's wife, Queen Guinevere. This scandal put their relationship to many tests. It left Arthur vulnerable, provided ammunition for his opposition, threw the adoption and implementation of Arthur's cultural reforms into jeopardy, and put his life at risk.

Seeking to distance himself from Guinevere for the sake of the king, Lancelot left Camelot on a series of quests. During one adventure, Lancelot was duped into thinking that he could have a rendezvous with Guinevere, but instead he impregnated a young woman named Elaine, who eventually gave birth to Galahad. Guinevere raged at what she thought was a betrayal, and Lancelot was driven mad by the conflict. He lived as a wild man for several years before being recognized by Elaine and taken in to recover.

Through the tumult, Arthur fought invaders from the outside and schemers from the inside and attempted to tame a fractured country. Using his authority and resources, Arthur used Might for Right as his noble strategy to achieve Equal Justice, his final objective.

It was a struggle, however, to find the best methods and tactics to steer civilization toward reform. He decided to channel the energies of his restless knights toward a quest for the Holy Grail. Nearly all failed to reach their goal. One of the three to behold the treasure was the very holy and pure Sir Galahad, Lancelot's son. Lancelot, who had spent so much effort trying to overwhelm and counteract his sins with good deeds, was not allowed to receive the chalice.

After the quest for the Holy Grail, Arthur faced great treachery on the part of his own family. Mordred, seeking revenge against his father, trapped Lancelot in Guinevere's bedroom, thus forcing Arthur to prosecute Lancelot along with his own wife. Lancelot rescued Guinevere at the moment before her execution but, in the heat of that battle, killed Gareth and Gaheris—the unintentional victims of collateral damage. Arthur pursued the fleeing Lancelot into France, where, eventually, the Pope's emissary negotiated a settlement. Guinevere returned to Camelot, but Gawaine insisted on continuing the siege against Lancelot to avenge the deaths of his two brothers.

While Arthur was occupied with Lancelot, Mordred falsely informed the kingdom that Arthur was dead. As a result, Guinevere was forced to marry Mordred. However, when word of the coup reached Arthur, Gawaine and Lancelot joined the king in hurrying back to England. The old and weary king, the night before he was forced to kill his son and then face his doom, hoped to ensure the continuation of his reforms by quickly communicating some pearls of wisdom to a young page, Tom Malory. Arthur exacted a promise from this unlikely vessel of hope that he would not seek battle but rather would stay alive. Thus, the king was able to keep the light of his vision shining into the next generation and all the generations that followed.

CHAPTER 1

FINDING MERLIN: GETTING A MENTOR AND PLUGGING THE BRAIN DRAIN

The most common description of Merlin is that of an elderly wizard with a long white beard, wearing a pointed hat and a flowing costume accented by stars and moons. He's synonymous with magic and sorcery. But Merlin's significance was not his ability to conjure or foretell the future. Above all else, this archetypal sorcerer (just look at how J. K. Rowling borrowed some elements from him to create Dumbledore in the wonderful *Harry Potter* series) was a mentor and adviser.

Why begin here with mentoring? For starters, it was something I wished for dearly when I was starting out. I had an amiable relationship with my boss and enjoyed the camaraderie of my team. I received advice here and there from some of the old-timers, but the real learning was up to me. The reality was that I could have solicited more and the organization could have provided more.

With the aid of his mentor, Arthur's life took on an entirely new direction; it was pivotal to his development and his future role of king. Today, too, coaching, teaching, and mentoring are pivotal points in determining directions and enhancing capabilities. In addition, programs or systems to help educate and engage employees are of critical importance to any modern enterprise because there's an ever-increasing amount of knowledge to impart, as well as the constant pressure to recruit and retain talented people.

England in the time of Arthur, like the land of business today, was ruled by a multitude of competing and many times ruthless rulers, and there were constant threats from external rivals. The baby Arthur, the rightful heir to King Uther Pendragon, was protected from his enemies by Merlin, who asked the good Sir Ector to raise him as a son. Known as the Wart in Ector's household, the youngster didn't go looking for a tutor. It was

Sir Ector's friend, Sir Grummore Grummersum, who broached the idea of a teacher for Arthur and for Ector's own son, Kay. At the same time, Merlin, who was moving through time in reverse and, thus, aware of the future, was awaiting Arthur.

Despite all the words of support for mentoring today, it does not happen nearly enough or with enough process. Many leaders may declare themselves mentors of their underlings, but this claim is often made after the employee has achieved successes to which the executive can point. There's no better way to success than to climb aboard a success already made or well on the way to achievement. It's success by association.

Unfortunately, there's a dearth of purposeful evaluation of potential talent among the workforce and mentoring relationships. Conversely, few junior staffers seek out mentors. This may be due to the timidity of the individual, a lack of good leadership and role models within the organization, or an organizational environment that suppresses interaction between levels. Merlin, however, gave clear permission to Arthur to speak up and be inquisitive; his mission was to educate, to expand Arthur's horizons, and to prepare him for challenges yet to be known.

"Would you mind if I asked you a question?"
"It is what I am for."[1]

To their credit, Ector and Grummore made a purposeful effort to find the boys a mentor, and Arthur was fortunate that a third party took an interest in making the connection between student and mentor. Instead of relying on local talent, Ector and Grummore cast the net widely, first by advertising the position and, later, by elevating the matter by making it a personal mission—a quest—to attract the right person.

"But even if you was to have a tutor," said Sir Ector, "I don't see how you would get him."
"Advertise," said Sir Grummore.
"I have advertised," said Sir Ector. "It was cried by the Humberland Newsman and Cardoile Advertiser."
"The only other way," said Sir Grummore, "is to start a quest."
"You mean a quest for a tutor," explained Sir Ector.
"That's it."[2]

Ector and Grummore played the role of a mentor connector, literally the MC/emcee of fostering mentoring introductions. Just as there are coordinators for internship programs, an MC within an organization could be a human resources professional or an executive with a passion for the development of talent within the organization.

This chapter is not meant to be a mentoring manual, but a good first step would be to establish some criteria or minimum requirements and audit both the potential pool of candidates and the mentors. A database could then help to connect the interests and expertise of executives with the rising stars.

It was all well and good that the adults—the MCs—in Arthur's life sought a tutor for him, but the future king was still a boy and lacked any insight into his own potential or the long-term benefit of an education. As we've all experienced in business or in our personal lives, things go down harder if they're forced upon us. "Because I said so," "Do it for your own good," or "Here's the way it's gonna be" are all-too-common "explanations." Not only are the teachings harder to accept, but we can also become bored, distracted, or resentful to the point of undermining the whole affair and dooming it to failure.

Arthur, being fairly pliable and deferential, at least went through the motions in his early dealings with Merlin. Yet, without having a personal stake in the outcome, without having input into the process, one can't offer commitment. It all becomes a "have to do," not a "want to do" or a "need to do."

> *"I think I ought to have some eddication," said the Wart. "I can't think of anything to do."*
>
> *"You think that education is something which ought to be done when all else fails?"*[3]

Mentoring can't be an afterthought or a vehicle for creating appearances, something that looks good on paper but, in fact, has no teeth. This cuts both ways, too. For the senior player, taking on the responsibility of mentoring should be considered thoughtfully. It's a commitment, not just something to boast about or an opportunity to "check the box," as many tend to do in so-called assigned-mentor relationships. (These inexpensive programs are like speed dating for mentors. The mentor-mentee relationship can be forced, with little connecting the two beyond a few prescribed criteria.) And, for the young manager, seeking a mentor should not be an exercise in brown-nosing or political climbing. It should be done with the honest intention of learning from the best that the organization has to offer.

Merlin was such a best-in-class individual. He was a visionary guide, in part, because he had already experienced the future. But Merlin didn't give away the secrets of the future or conjure a potion or wave a wand to give Arthur knowledge or insight. His power as a mentor was derived from his ability to use magical powers to expose Arthur to different walks of life, both human and nonhuman. He had Arthur walk the proverbial mile in someone else's shoes (or, in this case, something else's fins, talons, exoskeletal legs, wings, and paws). As a wizard, Merlin didn't need to bring Arthur to other parts of the world to experience the different religions, cultures, and customs of humankind. Merlin turned him into a fish, hawk, ant, goose, and badger—beings far more different and far more ancient with far more to tell the youngster. During these transfigurations, Arthur, as an impatient and immature boy, did not fully appreciate his lessons. He viewed them more as adventures and reprieves from his normal workaday world as the future squire to his adoptive brother, Kay, than as golden opportunities for learning.

> *"Could you turn me into an ant?"*
> *"They are dangerous."*
> *"You could watch with your insight, and turn me back again if it got too bad. Please turn me into something, or I shall go weak in the head."*[4]

While voicing his annoyance, Arthur blinds himself to the potential outcomes or the importance of his education. He's bored, and boredom, as noted above, can bring the best of intentions to a grinding halt. One strategy to mitigate this problem is to develop a plan or agenda. All projects need planning, and so does mentoring. Goals must be discussed (what will be achieved by the end of the relationship), resource requirements defined (what equipment, money, or other human resources will be needed), and expectations set regarding how much time can or can't be devoted to the mentoring relationship. Some relationships may be fairly open–ended, and others may revolve around specific projects. Either way, a mutual understanding must be set carefully and clearly.

> *"By the way," added the magician, stopping in the middle of his spell, "there is one thing I ought to tell you. This is the last time I shall be able to turn you into anything. All the magic for that sort of thing has been used up, and this will be the end of your education.*
> *"Do you think you have learned anything?"*
> *"I have learned, and been happy."*[5]

Merlin, brilliant but muddled, ends his mentorship with a "by the way," not a planned exit. Merlin doesn't disappear from Arthur's life as abruptly as we may think from this conversation, however. He remains at court as an adviser for a time following Arthur's coronation. Similarly, a mentor shouldn't suddenly go absent from the relationship. The formal part of the pact may be over, but there's every reason to stay in touch, bounce some ideas around, or get a reality check every now and then.

In response to Merlin's query about what he learned, Arthur signals some sort of undefined fulfillment. He was happy to receive the attention, he was grateful for the occasional diversion from the drudgery he was seemingly condemned to, but how much was he supposed to learn? He never knew the big picture; he didn't know what Merlin's original goals were. Without an expectation, without knowing what he was supposed to find at the finish line, he's not sure how to measure his own success.

Setting expectations includes defining the limits of the help or advice that will be provided. When Arthur took the form of a fish, he had to learn how to move and navigate in the multidimensional space of water. He sought and received help from a nearby fish, but he also received a warning: help was fine, but one cannot always rely on it. Indeed, the best kind of help is that which aids in the development of self-sufficiency and expertise.

> *"For this once," said a large and solemn tench beside his ear, "I will come. But in the future you will have to go by yourself. Education is experience, and the essence of experience is self-reliance."*[6]

After Arthur became king, he received a similar warning from Merlin. Merlin knew that he and Arthur would eventually be taking divergent paths and that the king had to begin asserting his own style upon his reign.

> *"That's more like it. Stand up for yourself, that's the ticket. Asking advice is the fatal thing. Besides, I won't be here to advise you, fairly soon."*[7]

But why would Merlin declare that seeking advice is fatal? Shouldn't we be resourceful? Don't good leaders and managers involve others in their research, analysis, and decision making? What happened to "two heads are better than one" and the "collective IQ?" Aside from Merlin knowing that Arthur had a superior sense of right and wrong and would use his power wisely, we need to remember that Arthur was a king in a long-ago land. There was an expectation then that kings would rule with absolute authority. Moreover, as we'll see in Chapter Three, he was on the verge of setting his kingdom on an entirely new course toward tolerance and justice. His vision was such a radical departure from historical norms that he would have risked weakening or destroying his initiatives if he asked for advice. Sometimes an "executive decision" is the only means to arrive at a new destination.

There are other examples of mentoring in *The Once and Future King*, including the relationship between Lancelot and his uncle, Gwenbors (affectionately called Uncle Dap). Teaching Lancelot all he knew, Uncle Dap helped his nephew achieve his goal of being the best knight in the world. Learning by example, Lancelot himself became a mentor after some time as a full-fledged knight.

"He favours the young knights, and tries to help them win the spurs."[8]

There are also a series of incidents brought to us through the delightful intersection of yet another legend from the English past, Robin Wood. (We learn from T. H. White that historians and writers got it wrong and inappropriately renamed him Robin Hood.) When planning the mission to rescue the kidnapped Friar Tuck and others from the evil Morgan le Fay (Arthur's half-sister), Robin rehearses his band over and over until each move is committed to memory.

When he had finished his speech, which was listened to in perfect silence, an odd thing happened. He began at the beginning and spoke it from start to finish in the same words. On finishing it for the second time, he said, "Now captains," and the hundred men split into groups of twenty . . .

They were repeating the speech, word for word. Probably none of them could read or write, but they had learned to listen and remember.[9]

This example shows how a perceptive and compassionate mentor adapts his or her style to ensure that the teachings connect with the recipient. Robin knew his audience: his merry men were committed to their cause and skilled in their art, but they were mostly illiterate. Whereas Merlin relied on an experiential, hands-on approach, Robin focused on listening techniques and repetition to educate his team. We also observe that instructions were given first in a large group and then repeated in smaller teams; everyone got the same set of directions from the boss, which were then reinforced in the working groups.

The 1967 movie *The Dirty Dozen* (based on the novel by E. M. Nathanson) used a similar method to good effect when the rag-tag army squad of murderous felons repeatedly recited the 16 steps of the plan in preparation for their assault on the German high command in a Nazi-occupied chateau.

Whatever the means or methods, the goal of mentoring/coaching/teaching is to transfer expertise, to feed the next generation so that they can bring themselves and their work to as high or a higher level than the mentor had achieved.

But everything has its limits, and the limits of mentoring are also mentioned in the story. In a passage describing the growing wisdom and maturing of Arthur's wife, Queen Guinevere (at the ripe old middle age of 22), we learn that there are crucial intangibles—life's experiences—that can't be written into any lesson or handed down in any oral tradition.

There is a thing called knowledge of the world, which people do not have until they are middle-aged. It is something which cannot be taught to younger people, because it is not logical and does not obey laws which are constant. It has no rules.[10]

Younger professionals may not always appreciate the importance of experience. (I certainly didn't believe it in my earlier days, and just think about how many billions of children across the globe and across time have spat out the words "You don't understand!" to their parents.) In the ego of youth, many believe that the weight of experience can be overwhelmed with terrific intelligence and inborn talent. But we know that intelligence and capability can't trump experience. It takes experience to complete the mentoring equation: capabilities + insights + experiences allow the individual to both excel in and exert influence over his or her domain, in whatever form that may be.

In some cases, the student can become the teacher or, at least, an expert in his or her own right. Some mentors, more experienced and self-confident, welcome the growth and independence of their students. Others feel overwhelmed or suspicious when they are overtaken by an upstart.

For there can be no greater bitterness in the world than this: That a man shall be betrayed by one to whom he himself hath given the power of betraying him.[11]

Merlin was beguiled and then betrayed by the beautiful Vivien, daughter of the king of Northumberland, who served in the court of Queen Morgan le Fay. After Vivien learned everything she could from the queen, she craved still more. She set her sights on Merlin, the top man in her chosen field of sorcery. She drew volumes of information from him, including his principal weakness, that he could see the future of others but not his own. Craving sole possession of the top rung of wizardry, the student locked her mentor away in a cave.

Vivien entered the mentoring relationship under false pretenses and violated the requirements of good intentions and open and honest dialogue. Misplaced trust, as Merlin found, can have dangerous consequences.

Whereas Vivien viewed Merlin as a rival, we can see a different potential landmine at the opposite end of the relationship spectrum. The perception of favoritism can create jealousies and undermine the credibility of both the mentor and the mentee. There should be abso-lutely no *quid pro quo* stated or implied other than the commitment of time to achieve some agreed-upon learning goals. No one should want questions raised about the nature of the connection between the two parties. Gossip and rumors are more than distractions; they can be vicious, time-stealing, reputation-killing scourges to people and their organizations. What may be one person's favoritism, however, may turn out to be another's sour grapes.

"Merlyn does everything for you, but he never does anything for me."[12]

I have no doubt that complaints about differential treatment have existed since the dawn of humankind. Sure, complaining can alienate. It can brand us as disloyal. It can lead to stress and, some say, even shorten our life. Yet, there is often a message in the misery. After all, complaining is a form of communication, and, like any exchange, we need to know our audience. For all of us, there is an ongoing need to read between the lines. It's a neces-sary procedure that leaders must undertake to truly understand the totality of the person. Thus, we could consider categorizing complainers as:

- *Attention Seekers.* This may be the largest category of complainers—those who may have some unfulfilled emotional need for attention. If there's an unmet need, it might be worth exploring what caused the void, why it may not be getting filled, and what it might take to make a permanent (or at least a long-lived) repair.
- *Terminally Annoying.* Some people may be just hardwired to whine. They have to gain some insight, recognize the behavior, and devise some tactics to overcome the impulse. Otherwise, we have to cope with it or tune it out.
- *Clinically Complicated.* Some complainers would be better categorized as patients with neuroses. Guiding them toward some medical or psychological intervention might be indicated.

- *Pressure Cookers*. It can be a scary situation to witness a usually even-keeled person erupting into a complaining rant. It's unexpected and it's out of character. These complainers lack a relief valve that can episodically vent some steam. They need to understand that communicating in a timely manner and to the right person will not diminish their likability and will, in fact, create better relationships.
- *Crowd Followers*. Due to a lack of confidence or an eagerness to fit in and be accepted, some people will take the lead of others and join in on the complaining. They need to think more about which crowd they want to be aligned with.
- *Signal Senders*. In my experience, there is an underappreciated group that may be making an actual, yet inept, attempt to communicate an issue or send an alert, but the message is interpreted as a complaint. Rather than brushing it off, it may be worth investigating the motivation or intent.

We could and should be reading more into the whines, moans, and carping we hear each day, but, as Freud might have said, sometimes a complaint is just a complaint. So, was Kay just a spoiled little brat, having a bad day and feeling cranky or simply annoying? Or, was part of his protest about the special attention paid to Arthur a different kind of signal, one that he couldn't quite articulate? Like so many matters, to some degree it was probably all of the above. The bottom line is that you can complain all you want, but most times, you won't get what you don't ask for. Don't be shy in seeking your answers.

Leaders—good leaders—want the most capable people working with and for them. If the leader has a role in the young worker's success, it contributes to his or her own reputation. It reinforces his or her status in the organization as a builder, as a team-oriented leader whose mission— the success of the enterprise and its people—is on clear display.

Merlin and Arthur weren't the first famous pairing, of course. There have been apprentices and disciples throughout history, and many have followed since. In addition to the countless clergy and craftsmen who learned from their elders, we have many modern-day examples that cut across business, society, music, and sports. Just look at airline moguls Sir Frederick (Freddie) Laker and Sir Richard Branson, civil rights leaders Dr. Benjamin E. Mays and Dr. Martin Luther King Jr., music icon Berry Gordy Jr. with Smokey Robinson and Diana Ross, and Eddy Merckx, a five-time Tour de France winner mentoring Lance Armstrong, a seven-time winner. A group in Canada, Peer Resources, maintains a virtual Mentor Hall of Fame.[13] In the United States, there is a National Mentoring

Month (in January) that focuses on children and their development. And, there's even a mentoring group called MERLIN, the Madison (Wisconsin) Entrepreneur Resource, Learning, and Innovation Network.[14]

A set date to acknowledge and publicize mentoring is great—anything to drive some action is certainly welcomed. Yet, these activities must occur year-round. It's obvious that on a regular basis, we need to feed the brains of our employees, help them to become more skilled and confident, and keep them engaged with the organization. Boredom and apathy are powerful determinants in an employee's future success or in a decision to stay or leave.

There's also a huge risk and a huge cost attached to the another side of the employment coin. Not investing in an adequate program to promote ongoing learning and knowledge transfer could easily result in critical knowledge loss, business downtime, and increased recruiting costs. And it's not just the lack of a training or mentoring program that puts the organization at risk. Knowledge retention becomes a critical issue when the business faces a downsizing or a slew of departures or retirements. Institutions representing diverse interests, such as Delta Airlines, the National Aeronautics and Space Administration, Shell Oil, and Siemens, have instituted critical job-loss programs to address the brain-drain issue. Unfortunately, these initiatives—some as simple as having the veteran players use online tools to document processes and procedures—are often launched in response to a crisis situation after significant damage has already been inflicted on the organization.

Institutions should support teaching, coaching, and mentoring, but not all organizations are capable of supporting a formal mentoring program. Rather than be intimidated by the time or logistical issues, organizations can start small, even if it's as basic as a shadowing program where mentees act as flies on the wall, soaking up the observations.

". . . set you in the mews for the night so that you can talk to the others. That is the way to learn, by listening to the experts."[15]

Before being allowed to take wing, Merlin ensured that Arthur had time to learn and interact with the experts (birds of prey, in this case), like ground school for pilots before they take control of an aircraft. As long as a program allows watching, listening, asking, and doing, you'll have a more successful organization.

Mentoring doesn't need to be terribly sophisticated, overly compli-cated, or worthy of a profile or case study in a business publication to be effective. Nor do the formal mentoring relationships need to be forever.

But mentoring does need to be more than just the assignment of a corporate "buddy" to a new employee, someone who is merely a glorified tour guide to point out the bathroom and cafeteria on the worker's first day of work. The effort needs compatible individuals, and learning goals must go beyond knowing the floor plan.

In order to expose a greater number of employees to a limited number of mentors, time limits can be put in place. Whatever the program, it needs a framework, a mutual commitment, and tools to evaluate success. Whatever the form or format, mentoring helps to accelerate the acquisition of experience and, thus, the accelerated development of thoughtful, productive leaders.

CAMELOT WISDOM:

- Because an individual's potential is much more fully realized with the help of a wise and creative mentor, it's crucial for organizations to find a way to make mentoring a reality.
- Although advertising, such as what Sir Ector and Sir Grummore attempted, may not be the best approach, it's important to have a system to connect the right mentor with the right mentee.
- Merlin ensured that coaching/teaching/mentoring was not an optional activity. A consequence of not engaging and supporting employees may be a catastrophic brain drain of knowledge and experience. This could produce a cascade of effects, including potential business loss and costs to recruit, retain, and retrain staff.
- There is no one-size-fits-all approach to mentoring; there is a wide spectrum of potential parameters and initiatives that can translate into successful outcomes. Nor is a mentoring program a reward-related activity or a personality contest; it should be a fixed (but not forced) method of connecting compatible individuals and evaluating and promoting talent.
- Understanding the student (or coworker, friend, or relative) means reading between the lines; there may be a hidden message inside a comment or complaint.
- Mentoring must be purposeful and authentic. A mentoring relationship should come with an agreement between the involved parties on terms and objectives.

CHAPTER 2

BECOMING A FISH: WALKING IN ANOTHER'S SHOES AND GAINING EMPATHY

As we saw in the previous chapter, the young Arthur was turned into a variety of nonhuman beings by his mentor, Merlin, in order to learn the ways of the world and to prepare him for his destiny as king. Through Merlin's magic, Arthur was able to experience some of the everyday struggles for survival, including the importance of finding a common ground for communication. He was even able to feel the nuances of different forms of joy and sadness.

These transfigurations into fur, fin, and feather (and bug) were a big part of the magician's mentoring technique, a technique of turning the learning process into an adventure. Arthur's immersion learning took place in the environments where these creatures lived. These were sometimes dangerous places where Arthur had to observe, adapt, and think quickly in his new surroundings. His abilities to react swiftly and smartly weren't just important; they were essential. Arthur's observational powers and quick wits enabled him to save his own life while being attacked by a hawk (while he was in bird form) and, as an ant, getting caught in the middle of a war between two colonies. Later, as king, Arthur would leverage these experiences not just to better understand and connect with others, but also to win over doubters and adversaries and to prevail in decisive battles against larger armies.

There were doubters and adversaries within his own family. Some of Arthur's nephews, raised by his crazed half-sister, leaned toward him, while others leaned away from him and his plans. (Gawaine was the most loyal, while Agravaine and Mordred plotted against Arthur.) The king realized that it wasn't as much a matter of ideology as it was the indoctrination they received from their oppressive and emotionally withholding mother.

"The real matter with them is Morgause, their mother. She brought them up with so little love or security that they find it difficult to understand warm-hearted people themselves. They are suspicious and frightened."[1]

Arthur noted the fear his nephews felt. Morgause was mentally ill, but she was still their mother; despite the toxicity of the relationship, it's hard to break that bond. He recognized that fear was a driver of bad behavior in his own foster brother, Kay. Kay's boasts, putdowns, and snubs, Arthur believed, were a result of his lack of confidence in himself and not a lack of brotherly love.

"He has to be proud because he is frightened."[2]

It was clear to Arthur that having the ability to understand other people (and the other creatures that inhabit the Earth), their circumstances, and their environments was not only nice and good, but important in other ways, too. He learned that one can achieve a huge competitive advantage. Who do people want to advocate for, fight for, or work for? Most often it is the person who takes an interest in them, recognizes their motivation, and feels their pains and their successes.

Indeed, just about everyone clamors for some understanding. But this cuts both ways: we want to be understood by others, and others want us to understand them. Yet, we may be losing our collective capacity to understand on an emotional level. A review of 72 studies conducted between 1979 and 2009 with nearly 14,000 U.S. college students showed a 40 percent decrease on a measure of empathy compared to their counterparts 20 or 30 years earlier.[3] If an emotional quotient is as important as an intelligence quotient, then this issue must be addressed urgently because "young adults today comprise one of the most self-concerned, competitive, confident, and individualistic cohorts in recent history."[4] The potential implications might be that if this population group won't make the time to worry about the long-term needs of their partners, associates, or employees, their relationships and their businesses will suffer.

To help propel greater comprehension and appreciation of others, there is a growing trend to create opportunities for role reversals. A number of companies have taken the step to bring down the barriers of communication and institutionalize this practice. For example, executives at companies like Continental Airlines, Loews Hotels, food marketer and distributor SYSCO, and the Walt Disney Company perform front-line or entry-level jobs at least once a year.

These job swaps, conceived as ways to learn from and connect to the front lines of the business, have caught the attention of the entertainment industry. The television show *Undercover Boss*, premiered in 2010 and tapped into the public's appetite for reality TV and the chance to see the CEO face the sometimes grimy reality, even if it's temporary.

Yes, this all helps to increase face time between management and staff, drive some positive public relations, and (for the less cynical) bolster morale. But there can be demonstrable enhancements to competitiveness and profitability, too. After some senior managers at DaVita, a provider of dialysis services, went through their immersion experience in 2007, CEO Kent J. Thiry observed, "The experience changes their view of the world. They are better leaders as a result."[5] Planning, scheduling, and training have all been affected by DaVita's "Reality 101" program.

These corporate programs have been organized and administered by management. On the other side of the labor coin, the Service Employees International Union in the United States has instituted a "Walk a Day in My Shoes" campaign: a challenge to engage candidates running for political offices. Some top political leaders have shadowed a variety of workers, including a school custodian, a nurse, a home care worker, and a teacher in the federally funded Head Start program.

Some of literature's and popular culture's well-known examples of walking in another's shoes don't originate from this foundation of purposeful intentions, however. Edward Tudor in Mark Twain's *The Prince and the Pauper* comes to realize that "kings should go to school to try their own laws at times, and so learn mercy" quite by accident. A similar lesson was learned when Eddie Murphy and Dan Aykroyd were forced into polar opposite worlds as part of a cruel (and hilarious) wager between two tycoons in the 1983 movie *Trading Places*. And besides *Undercover Boss*, there have been other reality TV shows like *Trading Spouses: Meet Your New Mommy*, *Now Who's Boss?*, and *Wife Swap*. Yet, many of the "teachable moments" come from staged dilemmas that result in sometimes squeamish moments geared for the entertainment of the viewers, and not so much for the edification of the participants.

Compassion or empathy, as we've all experienced, can be hard to find in books, film, and real life. As we've discussed, Arthur tried to use his emotional insights to help overwhelm some of the pangs of sibling rivalry that popped up occasionally with Kay. This, plus the boy's desire for some company on his adventures led him to ask Merlin to extend the opportunity of an animal world adventure to Kay. Although Arthur was motivated by doing the right thing (as well as some self-interest), Merlin refused his request.

*"Perhaps what is good for you might be bad for him. Besides, remember he
has never asked to be turned into anything."*[6]

Merlin's response has great meaning to us, too. We can always guess
or assume what might be best for another, but we don't see the world
through their eyes. We don't carry their experiences, their fears, or their
desires. Even the most empathetic among us cannot fully understand
another person. So, in addition to being careful of what you ask for
yourself, be careful of what you ask for another person.

As much as we'd like to think so, we don't always know what's best
for others—or even ourselves, sometimes. When I was promoted into a
position of leading people who were formerly peers in the organization,
I was confronted with the realization that one friend was not performing
well. I found myself rewriting some of his memos and reports and conducting the follow-up on some of his assignments. I was protecting him.
Finally, I understood that I wasn't doing either of us any favors. I was
running myself ragged, and his work didn't improve. That's when I got
the religion of coaching and mentoring.

Thinking that we know best isn't thinking at all. In presentations or
interviews, our default setting is usually already dialed in to what we
want to say, what we know, and what we're comfortable communicating.
But there may be a large gap between the words and tone of what we
would like to use and the words and tone that are most appropriate for
the audience that must be addressed. Knowing your audience and knowing
your environment are crucial considerations. (We'll return to this in
Chapter Eight.)

Most of the animal-world adventures that Merlin set before the
young Arthur revolved around lessons of discipline, critical thinking,
and the waste and horror of war. But Arthur's first foray into an alien
environment was when he entered the world of the moat surrounding
Ector's castle.

*The Wart found it difficult to be a new kind of creature. It was no
good trying to swim like a human being, for it made him corkscrew and
much too slowly. He did not know how to swim like a fish.*[7]

This was a strange and uneasy situation for the young, uninitiated
boy. He had to reorient himself to a dense, multidimensional water
environment—and new environments or situations frequently require
new thinking and new solutions. But what was it that Merlin was
really attempting to teach his charge? As we've seen, he was honing

his strategic thinking and creative approaches to problem solving and decision making. More importantly, though, Arthur was being prodded to survey the world through different sets of eyes. Arthur was already an honest and good-natured boy, and he was developing a higher order of compassion, empathy, and tolerance. These were some of the essential ingredients that he needed to sew into the fabric of his being in order to develop and deploy his yet-to-come societal reforms.

The worlds of the animals taught much, but there was also plenty for Arthur to learn from his human surroundings. Even so, without Merlin's mentoring, Arthur's path through life would have taken an altogether different trajectory. His was an authoritarian world with clear hierarchies and high boundaries between the levels of society. And with no one in the household knowing of Arthur's noble birth, he would not have been expected to rise above the predetermined occupation of squire, a knight's attendant.

When Arthur became the squire to his adopted brother, Kay, the world he knew, the interactions he enjoyed, shifted abruptly; he was an instant victim of the old class system. No longer an equal, Arthur felt betrayal and frustration. It no longer mattered that they were raised as brothers and friends. The wedge pushing them apart was molded by their society, but it was Kay—too weak, too close-minded, and too greedy—who glorified the differences. The key point for Kay was that doing what was expected was more important than doing what was right.

> . . . *Kay did not care to associate with the Wart any longer on the same terms, because he would need to be more dignified as a knight, and could not afford to have his squire on intimate terms with him.*[8]

We all have to make efforts to recognize and resist Kay's mistake. Doing what's right may sound risky, and under certain circumstances in some environments—at work, at home, or among friends—it might be. But on the whole, it's a safe and wise choice. In your business dealings and in your relationships with friends and family, doing the right thing leads to trust, credibility, and respect. These principles are some core pieces of the foundation of leadership, the magnets with which you attract the support of your business associates, clients, and loved ones. Even if you are criticized, you'll always have the satisfaction of knowing that you were right! The bottom line is that "expected" is for the ordinary, the mediocre; "right" is for the courageous, the outstanding.

In the case of Kay and Arthur, Arthur chose not to rebel against the status quo; pushing the point too hard would have wrecked any chance of maintaining their brotherhood. So, if the first part of Kay's mistake was giving in to expectation, then the second part was not remembering or cherishing his roots: who he once was, who his supporters were, and where he found his strength. In a different context, we see this in today's "trophy wife" phenomenon. Of course, people do sometimes drift apart, but, in many cases, we see "root rot"—relationships deemed disposable when wealth, power, influence, and/or celebrity are on the rise. Kay's root rot was evident when he unkindly reminded Arthur that he was not a "proper son" because his parentage was uncertain.

> . . . *Kay had taught him that being different was wrong.*
> *Besides, he admired Kay and was a born follower. He was also a hero-worshipper.*[9]

This quote also notes that Arthur was keen to be liked and included, like a puppy looking for approval. This approval-seeking boy seems far removed from the inspiring hero-king we observe later, which brings us to another point. Things change: our times, our circumstances, our fortunes, and our relationships. We can ignore it, acknowledge it, or embrace it and move forward.

Like people, organizations may end up in very different places from where they started. Rebranding has become more commonplace as corporations and people adapt to changing needs and conditions. Wire and Plastic Products, making shopping baskets, became the global advertising and public relations conglomerate WPP. Coleco, originally the Connecticut Leather Company, moved from shoe leather to plastic pools to video games and consoles to the line of Cabbage Patch Kids dolls until it was sold off to Hasbro. Diebold, an industry leader in ATMs and electronic voting machines, was first a manufacturer of safes and locks. And Wipro Limited, the giant information-technology services company, was once Western India Vegetable Products. Sometimes the changes can be a little less revolutionary and a little more evolutionary. AOL was first Control Video Corporation and sold subscriptions for online video gaming. Apple was known as Apple Computer before the introduction of its iPhone.

In politics, we've seen similar reinventions and transformations. In the United States, for example, the White House has been occupied by an actor, a baseball team owner, and an owner of a clothing store. Other presidents have had occupations that ranged from farmer to general.

Changes like these occur sometimes by chance and sometimes through a dedicated plan. They can play out at a glacial pace or strike like an avalanche. Whatever the mechanism, people and organizations need to promote and maximize their flexibility to move beyond the expected and the disappointments, and around roadblocks or other changing conditions. Without a belief that such changes are possible, we severely limit our choices and our ability to succeed in all theaters of opportunity.

Opportunities for change and growth increase with the number of relationships we forge. With his innate decency, sharpening mind, and growing empathy, Arthur unknowingly made friends and allies as he moved through his young life. Merlin understood this, of course. He knew that learning was an investment in time—his and Arthur's. In *Grooming, Gossip, and the Evolution of Language*, Robin Dunbar pointed out that even primates put the necessary time into relationships. The more time spent, the stronger the bonds. "If grooming is the cement that holds alliances together, then the more time you devote to grooming your ally, the more effective that alliance will be," he said. "And, since alliances will be proportionately more important to you the larger the group gets, it makes sense to invest even more time in grooming your allies."[10]

The lessons of the animals led to a big and unexpected pay-off for Arthur: his successful encounter with the sword in the stone. Hearing of the tournament called to determine who shall have a chance to pull the sword, Arthur's family traveled to the big event in London. Anyone knows that you need to show up at a tournament with your sword, but Kay forgot his at the inn where they were all staying. He sent his squire, Arthur, to fetch it. Finding the room containing Kay's sword locked, Arthur went to the church square, where the fateful sword seemed to be the only one immediately available. This sword would make an acceptable substitute if he could pry it from its two-tiered scabbard of anvil and rock. Lifting the weapon was not an easy feat, and Arthur was not successful right away. It was at that moment that all of Arthur's different encounters with the animals—his lessons and learnings—came into focus. These weren't disparate interactions. Rather, his experiences combined and synergized into understanding and strength, enabling him to jump the rails of his expected life onto a royal track.

> All around the churchyard there were hundreds of old friends.
>   They loomed around the church wall, the lovers the helpers of the Wart, and they all spoke solemnly in turn.
>   . . . all, down to the smallest shrew mouse, had come to help on account of love. Wart felt his power grow.

"Fold your powers together, with the spirit of your mind, and it will come out like butter."[11]

Arthur persisted with the sword in the stone until he drew upon his collected learnings to finally seize it. It was the diversity of inputs from a diversity of creatures that aided his success. How wrong Kay was! He made Arthur feel ashamed because he was different; Arthur was made to feel that being different was somehow wrong. It's clear that we need differences, we need competing views and opinions, and we know that good ideas can come from anywhere.

Using our own collected experiences, we are able to view issues from different perspectives, evaluate information, synthesize it, expand upon it, and, ultimately, solve problems. We all know that the most important things in life or business don't come easily, and sometimes repetition or a change in strategy is required. In this story, Arthur did both: he persevered and he added new elements to his approach to the task.

Despite our best efforts, though, important lessons can be forgotten. (Doesn't it seem that the important information is forgotten more often and more completely than the useless trivia and factoids we can never seem to erase?) When we can recall the relevant information, it may have an inchoate quality; the precision is lost with the commingling of other memories and the passage of time. The ability to translate an experience or skill to other circumstances or environments might be hampered as well.

Arthur lapsed occasionally in this regard. He lost touch with what he had learned during his transformations when discussing a victory on the battlefield with Merlin; Arthur's famous empathy and compassion were swept away by his boyish fascination with war. He was caught up in the thrill, the glory, of battle and was blind to the human cost.

"It was a jolly battle, and I won it myself, and it was fun."
"How many of your kerns were killed?"
"It was not fun, then. I had not thought."
"The tally was more than seven hundred. They were all kerns, of course. None of the knights were injured, except the one who broke his leg falling off the horse."
"I ought to have thought of the people who had no armour."[12]

Merlin recast the picture of the battle for Arthur and made him question the leadership dogma and the inequalities embedded in his society. Is one human life worth more than another? Is he not in charge of all the peoples of the realm? Arthur knew right away that he had made a horrific mistake—one with a price of over 700 lives. He was king but still a boy. He had evolved as a person with the help of Merlin and the animals but was still human in every fallible sense of the word.

It's important to note that warriors, too, can have empathy. This is somewhat different from what Sun Tzu, the Chinese general, wrote centuries before Arthur. In his widely admired and cited *The Art of War*, he wrote, "If you know others and know yourself, you will not be imperiled in a hundred battles." The differentiating point is between knowing (the intellectual component) and feeling (the emotional component).

But Lancelot had a sort of methodical consideration for people—he was sensitive to things which they might be feeling, or might be likely to feel.[13]

War is cold and brutal. Yet the ability for commanders to know and to feel is a strategic asset. What's going through the mind of the enemy and of our own troops? How far can we push their body and their psyche? There's a reason why the military doesn't hire their generals and admirals from the outside. They must have walked in the soldier's boots and slept in the sailor's bunk. Lessons need to be lived so that they can become experiences.

We've heard over and over that we must learn by doing and that we must learn from our own mistakes. Organizations have, at least in words, grown to accept the inevitability of mistakes. Some encourage them, believing that some decision, even a bad one, is better than no decision at all.

Living with this mindset is one thing in the business world, but it's every parent's nightmare. As the chief executive of the family unit, we want to pass along our wisdom—all the dos and don'ts—to our children. Advice, guidance, and role-modeling are all essential, but the reality, of course, is that they must live their own lives. Just as our early encounters with life and nature help to finish the hardwiring in our brains after birth, our experiences become a growing network of wired connections that enable us to utilize the knowledge from a past situation and make good decisions in a different circumstance.

The connections we make and the learnings we gain cannot stop at an arbitrary place along our career paths. They cannot, and must not, stop. Recall the role-reversal programs from earlier in this chapter. Before reaching the top rungs, we often see young professionals and middle managers acquiring experience and perspective offered through rotational programs—getting a chance to test-drive other roles and responsibilities—at many corporations. (In some cases, there is no choice offered: if you want to advance at the company, you'll need to spend a couple of years in various assignments, such as sales, marketing, or business development.) Moving further up the ladder might entail longer-term commitments at an affiliate or divisional operation and, maybe, at an outpost abroad before coming back to the home office.

In the absence of a Merlin in our lives, we need to make these opportunities happen. If what you think you need isn't offered, go make some noise. Seek it, suggest it, and agitate for it. We can turn ourselves into fish if we take the initiative to make our needs and desires for learning known to the decision makers and MCs in the organization. And, we can help those who ought to be turned into fish by becoming an MC and advocating for investment in training and mentoring.

CAMELOT WISDOM:

- While reading and listening can bring much knowledge, Merlin helped to show Arthur that some lessons simply needed to be lived so that they could become experiences that embedded into his character and decision-making processes.
- Understanding others delivers a competitive advantage in gaining loyalty and in winning over doubters and adversaries. Arthur could not have wrested the sword Excalibur from the stone and become king if he had not learned and gained strength from the ordinary.
- Doing the right thing and acting with compassion and empathy lead to trust, credibility, and respect: core necessities for long-term, productive leadership. "Right" is for the courageous, the outstanding. Doing only the expected is for the ordinary, the mediocre.
- People must not be collected like trophies or disposed of casually. Building relationships takes time and effort. The more time spent, the stronger the bonds.
- A lack of insight or perspective, or losing touch with past lessons learned, can lead to serious or deadly consequences (in Arthur's case, the loss of over 700 foot soldiers).
- Learning does not, and should not, stop; people and organizations must evolve to address changing needs and environments.

CHAPTER 3

Might for Right: Developing a Plan with Mission, Vision, and Values

When Arthur became head of state, he had to quickly define and defend his administration and put his own mark of leadership on the kingdom. He was driven to act like any modern chief executive or elected official. Today, few chief executives take control of an organization and say, "We can't improve" or "There's no sense in making any changes." From an ego desire to leave a legacy or a mandate from the board of directors to shake things up, you can usually count on a new chief executive to make changes. And not changes that dribble out over time. Eager to confirm the wisdom of his or her elevation to the top post, new leaders will often communicate their 30- or 100-day plan, demonstrating their ability to take charge with decisive, swift action.

We are taught that power is the key to success and wealth, and that the powerful are in control. Power can be mental, physical, or political. Whatever the source or sources, we all tend to want it; we want to accumulate it and move up in the world. As we've seen from countless examples in history or in our daily lives, power (old or newly acquired) can be thrilling and empowering but also potentially intoxicating and blinding. The sayings about being drunk with power or how power corrupts were coined with good reason.

Clearly, Arthur was not blinded by power (though he was blinded, like all humans, by other things, as we'll see later). Despite all the talk about compassion and empathy in the previous chapter, Arthur didn't always see or appreciate the brutality of injustice, of power-grabbing and the way one class of citizens was valued over another. Viewing the aftermath of battle, Merlin helped Arthur to realize that the might of his forces was being wasted and, worse, was tearing the country and its people, literally, apart.

"Their turbulence does not cost them anything themselves because they are dressed in armour—and you seem to enjoy it too. But look at the country. Look at the barns burnt, and dead men's legs sticking out of ponds, and horses with swelled bellies by the roadside, and mills falling down, and money buried."[1]

Although Merlin was commenting on the slaughter of the peasants, there's a lesson here, too, about a different kind of termination: the dismissal of employees following a merger or acquisition. Like the armor worn by kings and knights, the CEO and the management team are far better protected from market downturns than the rank-and-file employees. Some negative consequences aren't at the whim of the marketplace, however. Such self-inflicted wounds might come as a result of a poorly conceived merger, acquisition, or product strategy. Many times, these are rational and well engineered, yet there are too many examples where the motivation is ego and greed, pure and simple. There might be some magic woven into the record of King Arthur, but it hardly compares to the hocus-pocus business models and practices of companies like Enron and AIG.

With assurances of unique synergies and increased strength and cost savings, corporate marriages often fail to deliver a fraction of the promised benefit. These deals sometimes come with (usually very short-lived) power-sharing co-chairmen. Because these arrangements seem driven by the need to soothe some egos and not by any particular need of the business or its customers, they never seem to make sense. Generally, there's twice the pay but not twice the leadership. Employees and shareholders want and expect an ultimate authority to make the decisions and to be accountable for them. Arthur did not have a co-king. And, it's become a common refrain from the president-elect of the United States—no matter the party affiliation—that, when asked how the country should respond to this or that, they say, "There's only one president at a time."

The fight to acquire or to merge should not be the goal. An acquisition or a merger is a strategy to achieve something better, something greater than what the individual units can deliver. Just as war is a mechanism to achieve a political or policy goal, business deals, too, are a means to an end. It's what occurs after the deal that really counts. We need to keep our "eyes on the prize"—the long-term success of the new venture. It's not as sexy or media-friendly, but, as Peter Drucker, the legendary management and leadership guru, wrote, "The best plan is *only* a plan, that is, good intentions, unless it *degenerates into work.*"[2]

"I have got to vanquish them with their own weapons—they force it upon me, because they live by force—and then the real work will begin. This battle at Bedegraine is the preliminary, you see. It is after the battle that Merlyn is wanting me to think about."[3]

Rather than grow organically, some companies see no other way to expand their business other than pushing together dozens of sometimes quite disparate organizations. Some, like Berkshire Hathaway, GE, Hyundai, and Samsung, have found success. Companies like Tyco and Cendant have needed to break themselves apart into three and four pieces, respectively. Another serial acquirer, AMF (known originally as American Machine and Foundry), tried its hand at, among other things, nuclear reactors, tennis racquets, model airplanes, skis, motorcycles, power tools, and power-boats. Today, after shedding those businesses, it's an operator of bowling centers. Of course, there can be many reasons for failure, such as changing market conditions or poor management. The common ingredients for success, however, are (1) a keen understanding of the business proposition and (2) an ability to follow through with fast, fair, and financially rewarding integration. Anyone can make a deal; not just anyone can make the deal work to benefit all (and not just some) of the stakeholders.

"It was no good conquering the Dictator, unless you and the others do the civilizing part."[4]

Perhaps one of the biggest corporate disappointments was the combination of AOL and Time Warner. In a tremendous reversal of convictions several years after the merger announcement in 2000, a key engineer of the deal, AOL cofounder Steve Case, admitted that the hoped-for synergy of content and Internet delivery channel—"bricks and clicks"—was a failure and urged the company leadership to "take it apart."[5]

Prior to the merger, Time Warner had market cap of approximately $100 billion and AOL was valued at $163 billion. The promise was to create a new firm valued at $350 billion. Industry experts and mainstream, financial, and trade media all hailed the deal as "transformative," with rare exceptions.

Three years after the merger, in what is now regarded as one of the poster children for ill-conceived dot.com bubble-making, the market cap deflated to less than $40 billion. Seven years later, the market cap had clawed back, but far from even, to about $80 billion after management shifts and aggressive stock buybacks. The company tried to change perceptions by dropping AOL from its name but then finally called it quits in 2009 by splitting off the once-mighty Internet brand.

The business case for a deal must make sense, of course. But just as the numbers need to work and the products need to be complementary, so, too, must the people. David Harding and Ted Rouse of Bain & Company wrote, "Dealmakers gather reams of financial, commercial, and operational data. But they often pay scant attention to what we call human due diligence—understanding the culture of an organization, the roles that individuals play, and the capabilities and attitudes of its people."[6] Businesses are not inanimate objects. The careful evaluation and integration of people—the organization's most critical asset—set the foundation of the new venture on the proper footing. They enhance the power of the organization.

How people use their power—the power of their personality, their platform, their purse, or their police—helps to define the individual, the organization, and, ultimately, the society at large. Although much of who and what we are is hardwired into us, we do have the power to choose. We choose who we are, what we want to become, and with whom we want to deal. Do we want to define ourselves as bullies, a control freaks, or players of the patronage system? Or, as even-handed, approachable, or pragmatic?

Arthur had choices to make, too, as he ascended the throne. He could have taken any number of paths and internalized any number of outside recommendations to define his reign. Fortunately, he did not take the advice of Mr. P., the "King of the Moat" whom Arthur met while he was turned into a fish. Mr. P. had a philosophy of ruling that was quite the opposite of Arthur's sensibilities. He offers us a stark contrast to the fair-minded Arthur when he gives a forceful endorsement of civilization's *status quo*.

> *"There is only power. Power is of the individual mind, but the mind's power is not enough. Power of the body decides everything in the end, and only Might is Right."*[7]

Might is Right can work when you happen to be the "big fish" in the small pond (or, in this case, the moat)—the most imposing, dominant player in the realm. Throughout history, from tribalism to colonialism and imperialism, having power has been equated with the right to rule and subjugate others. Have you ever wondered why most aliens are portrayed as evil creatures in science fiction stories? The writers have simply extrapolated from the record of human history. Arthur had to swim against history's tide as he was exhorted to follow the expected path and take advantage of his position as the supreme ruler.

There's no doubt that in certain circumstances, however, more of the same is not only justified, it's required. Consistency and continuity do have their place, such as in the cases of health care delivery or the power grid. But taking a great leap forward in medical therapeutics or energy technology is different. That requires big, bold thinking.

Old England was not the time or place for more of the same, and Arthur saw his country, at war or under constant threat of war, at a crossroads. Unfortunately, he was not part of any succession plan. (We'll discuss this topic further in Chapter Thirteen.) He did not have a track record of leadership or as a turnaround artist. He had no transition period, no template, no guidelines, no base of support, and no experience that he could fall back on. Indeed, he started from behind. Even after he pulled the sword from the stone, the reaction to Arthur's ascendancy was not all positive. He was unknown and untested. He was a squire just moments before his triumphant pull and looked the part—the assistant just became the boss. The nobles did not embrace him, and, rather than rally around him, they sought to delay his coronation.

> *Some of the great lords had indignation that Arthur should be king, and put it off in a delay till the feast of the Pentecost.*
> *. . . they had no joy to receive no gifts of a beardless boy that was come of low blood. . . .*
> *. . . for it was great shame to all them to see such a boy to have a rule of so noble a realm as this land was.*[8]

What the people learned, however, was that the anticipation was much worse than the aftermath. What we conjure up, the horrible scenarios we play out in our minds, are usually much scarier or more harmful than the actual result. Sometimes, we can even be pleasantly surprised. After the resistance of the nobility faded and Arthur was crowned, there was a sense of relief that some positive change was at least possible.

> *They were sick of the anarchy which had been their portion under Uther Pendragon: sick of the overlords and feudal giants, of knights who did what they pleased, of racial discrimination, and of the rule of Might as Right.*[9]

Arthur was faced with a completely unexpected situation. Support began to flow his way (because word of his unique ability to pull the sword from the stone was spreading), but still, it must have been a dizzying time. Truly, his circumstances, his station in life, were turned upside down.

In these sudden and unusual situations, we have to rely on whatever smarts, savvy, experiences, and good judgment we have to literally make it up—our way, our plan—as we go along. I found myself improvising in my first leadership role as a professional not long after I landed a position after graduate school. My boss went out on a medical leave and left me in charge of a seven-person team. My only qualification was that I had the highest academic degree. Fortunately, I had a very forgiving group, and my management enrolled me in an in-house training program that provided some good nuggets of advice. The team understood and accepted the realities and were appreciative of my candid views. I made it clear that their expertise and experience were crucial to me and the continued progress of the group; equally clear were all of our roles, responsibilities, and accountabilities.

Arthur didn't have the same latitude; his only preparation came from what was hardwired into him and from the extraordinary set of lessons provided by an unusual man. Merlin had many wise things to tell Arthur, but he understood that the new king needed to come to his own conclusions. Arthur, not Merlin, had to own the decision and the consequences of that decision. Without ownership of the idea, as we see in the modern organization, effective, timely implementation will not occur. People need to see themselves—their inputs and their values—in the idea. The urgency to get things done, the passion of the pursuit, won't be found in an individual or in a team if they weren't in on the decision or, at least, informed of the rationale and decision-making process.

The process starts with asking a question. The answer sparks new questions until a tree of information is formed and a line of thinking can take shape. It's deliberate. It's thoughtful. It's a requirement for successful planning.

> *"Might isn't Right, is it, Merlyn?"*
> *"Aha!" replied the magician, beaming.*
> *"Is might right—and if not, why not, give reasons and draw a plan. Besides, what are you going to do about it?"*[10]

The use and misuse of power were in front of Arthur all of the time. Equally clear was the importance of national unification. The monarchy and the people needed a united country for the sake of internal harmony and for the sake of national defense. However, Arthur's sense of right and wrong dictated that unification could not be imposed by physical power or executive fiat alone.

"The destiny of Man is to unite, not to divide. If you keep on dividing you end up as a collection of monkeys throwing nuts at each other out of separate trees."
"Wrongs have to be redressed by reason, not by force."[11]

The problem, then, was how to create the common ground—a destination or a cause that could be a rallying point, bringing disparate groups together under a new banner and mutually enforcing the new order. The first step in this process was to set down the mission, vision, and values of the organization. In order to make the mission, vision, and values learnable and memorable, one must make them simple. Even a huge organization—a corporation, a government, or a kingdom—should be able to distill the concepts to a few sentences or phrases. General Electric CEO Jeffrey Immelt once said, "Every leader needs to clearly explain the top three things the organization is working on. If you can't, then you're not leading well."[12] Unfortunately, if you were to ask a typical employee in one of today's modern institutions to recite them, or even approximate them, they probably would be hard pressed. The reason might be an unfocused organization, poor communication from the top, or a basic lack of relevance to the employee. It's a disconnect that must be recognized and addressed.

Arthur's mission was to unite the country. His vision was a peaceful England. His values were to do what is right, not what was convenient or conventional.

"I don't think things ought to be done because you are able to do them. I think they should be done because you ought to do them."
"Why can't you harness Might so that it works for Right? I know it sounds nonsense, but, I mean, you can't just say there is no such thing. The Might is there, in the bad half of people, and you can't neglect it. You can't cut it out, but you might be able to direct it, if you see what I mean, so that it was useful instead of bad."[13]

Arthur's next steps were akin to developing a business plan, with the strategies and tactics he needed to make his mission, vision, and values a reality. This is the proper way to build toward the details of what actually gets implemented.

Getting started requires a plan. Indeed, you need a plan to make the plan. I have seen many instances where a group of well-intentioned, energetic (and/or undisciplined) people gather for a brainstorming session to kick off the process. They start shouting out their ideas in a spirited session and throwing around little toys to get the "creative juices" flowing while munching on snacks and drinking bottled water. As tempting as it might be to get those great tactics on the table (and show your colleagues how smart and creative you are), the tactics must come last.

You gain more credibility and effectiveness by first asking questions, not shouting out potential answers. Some of the basics consist of: When do we need to complete the task? What human and financial resources are available? Who is going to manage and evaluate the process? Who should be on the team, and what will be their roles and responsibilities?

The key question, of course, is: Do we have agreement on what we need to accomplish? Gaining concurrence on the informational, motivational, and behavioral objectives sets a common destination for the organization, team, or government: all eyes can visualize the intended goal. It also serves to define the populations who must be informed, motivated, and activated to make the dream a reality.

The number of stakeholders may be vast, however, and it may be time- and cost-prohibitive to attempt to reach them all. Thus, the list of targets requires prioritization. We need to think about: Who are the easiest to reach or to convince? Who are the most powerful, the most influential? Who can help influence an influencer? Audience analyses or audits, conducted every day by media, marketing, sales, advertising, and public relations professionals, can help select these segments for the maximal return on the program investment.

What is communicated to these groups comes from a refined set of messages—a set of three or four key points that must be repeated and reinforced throughout the life of the program. It's crucial that these messages do not contain what you want to say. The messages must reflect what your audiences need to hear. You must address their issues and concerns with the relevant facts in a language that is both persuasive and understandable.

In the first trial involving the anti-inflammatory drug Vioxx® in 2005 (where it was alleged that the drug's manufacturer, Merck, concealed health risks and was responsible for the death of Robert Ernst), the jury awarded $253 million to Ernst's widow, Carol. Why? Medical experts were there to explain on Merck's behalf and top attorneys probed, but the science went right over the heads of the jury. In an interview with *The Wall Street Journal*, a juror said, "We didn't know what the heck they were talking about."[14] The verdict was overturned in 2008, but the example is instructive. Have the right message (delivered by the right messenger, whenever possible) for the right audience.

Arthur directed his knights, the vehicles for his message delivery, to spread the latest word through the kingdom. The knights themselves were expected to model the behavior the kingdom hoped to see in this new age. It was beyond an expectation, actually. It was the Knight's Covenant, an unbreakable bond to carry forward the values of the kingdom.

> *[Arthur] charged them never to do outrageousity nor murder, and always to flee treason; also, by no means be cruel, but to give mercy unto him that asketh mercy, upon pain of forfeiture of their worship and lordship of King Arthur evermore for evermore; and always to do ladies, damosels, and gentlewomen succour, upon pain of death. Also, that no man take no battles in a wrongful quarrel for no law, nor for no world's goods.*[15]

Strategy development is the next step and arguably the hardest part of the process. It's the "How do we get from where we are to where we want to be?" You can look at it as if the "where we are" is a desolate island, devoid of any creature comforts. "Where we want to be" is the island with the resort, our destination. The strategy, then, is the bridge that connects the two. It's the platform, the roadway, and it's supported by the plan's tactics. (This is different from being strategic, which is the ability to look around the imaginary corner and make predictions that ultimately come true.) In Arthur's case, he was able to recast Mr. P.'s dictum of Might is Right into a new strategic imperative: Might for Right.

Today, the difficulty in finding the right path can be caused by a variety of factors, including being in a crowded market, having a product that lacks differentiation, or having audiences who might be jaded or combative. The strategy will also need to reflect the tolerance of the organization—whether or not you're working in a conservative organization, a cutting-edge entrepreneurial group, or someplace in between or in flux. And, depending on the needs, circumstances, and/or organizational environment, the strategy is sometimes straightforward nuts and bolts or creative and outside the box.

So, if the strategy is the bridge that takes us from where we are to where we want to be, then the tactics are the pillars that support the strategic roadway. If we laid down the tactics first, we'd have pillars in the water reaching up randomly in the hope of finding the bridge. Without that connection—tactics supporting the strategy that supports the objective—the effort won't have relevance to the audience, nor will the messages be memorable or durable.

Earlier, when we saw Arthur deliver his messages to his knights, we observed the "what"—the content of the communication. The "how" is the function of the tactics. We know that Arthur deployed his trusted emissaries to spread the reforms, but to make them embody the message, to energize the knights, he employed the tried and true carrot-and-stick method. Understanding that people are slow to change and that incentives are sometimes needed to spur the adoption of new concepts, he allowed them to maintain an outlet for their ingrained tendency to do battle. In a word, he found compromise.

> *"The knights in my order will ride all over the world, still dressed in steel and whacking away with their swords—that will give an outlet for wanting to whack . . .—but they will be bound to strike only on behalf of what is good."*[16]

In addition to the insight of channeling accepted and entrenched habits (swordplay and jousting) for the greater good, Arthur also understood that other factors would influence the success or failure of the plan's implementation. He accepted the inevitable—that there would be an uneven acceptance of his plan and that he'd need to rely on those who were still learning, still malleable. Thus, the roles and responsibilities of the knights could not and would not be equal.

> *"And the important thing,"* continued the king, who was getting wiser the more he thought, *"the most important thing, will be to catch them young. The old knights, the ones we are fighting against, will be mostly too old to learn."*
> *". . . they will be inclined to stick with the old habits."*[17]

Commenting that the older knights may hold fast to the past was recognition that there were issues to be managed moving forward. Arthur's instincts were correct, but not complete. Unfortunately, he wasn't able to take advantage of today's approach to issues and crisis preparedness with scenario planning, audience analysis, expert spokespersons, and crisis-response simulations to help him make informed choices about managing his knights.

The fact that the light of reform and fairness had not shown upon the people of the world in generations helped ensure that Arthur's plan would not be an instant success. Indeed, facts are sometimes quite useless (as we'll discuss further in Chapter Seven). On the one hand, Arthur needed to preserve and enhance the reputation and prestige of his knights. On the other, he wanted to draw the general population into the new age, not have them beaten into submission. Yet, few were clamoring for change. There was no real demand.

Arthur, however, found a way to break the logjam of human inertia and move the process forward. Understanding that emotion has the power to trump the facts, he found the common denominator: ego. He recognized the power and urges of the human mind to be part of an "in" group. Thus, he moved to create some cachet for his efforts by injecting a "must-have" attitude into the realm, and he helped to ensure that his reforms would be attractive and desirable to embrace.

"We shall have to make it a great honour, you see, and make it fashionable and all that. Everybody must want to be in."[18]

Arthur's brilliant insight resonates strongly with us today. Our consuming world revolves around cachet, with being "in" or being associated with the "it" person or product. We want the cars, the makeup, the clothes that are associated with celebrity, glamour, and cool. Many people even select their causes or charities based on what's fashionable.

Might for Right was a new and noble approach. It was an attempt to embed a new set of values and lay out a strategic approach for a country experiencing increasing disparity between the classes, in addition to the bloody, wasteful, internal, and external conflicts. It's often difficult to steer an organization to a new direction, but, with insight and planning, there's a chance that the initiative will have a positive impact that stands the test of time.

Modern organizations sometimes use their clout and resources to train their workforce to provide continual improvement, satisfaction, and retention and to acquire people, technologies, or companies that enhance the value and long-term prospects for the organization. Might for Right in an organization can also take the form of social marketing or corporate-responsibility programs. The act of getting something for something can mean that providing volunteers, financial or in-kind support, or the organization's good name for a worthy cause can pay dividends in the form of increased political capital, enhanced corporate reputation, positive publicity, the eventual development of a new market, and/or an aid to recruitment. One notable example is the $3-plus billion worth of medicines the pharmaceutical industry donates each year to help bolster its image.

Of course, the "because I say so" or "my way or the highway" method of leadership and management still has its place, though even the most obvious examples—the military, law enforcement, medicine, and sports—encourage on-the-spot decision making, depending on local events and conditions. Might for Right isn't necessarily the best underpinning for a successful corporate culture or the best path to achieve desired results. The people within the organization must understand and support the mission, vision, and values through their everyday communications, behaviors, and interactions. Today, workers see orientation videos and sign codes of conduct and sexual harassment policies when they join an organization—hardly the best way to communicate corporate values. Before the days of lawyers, human resource professionals, and ethics commissions, Arthur took visible steps to both set the standards he needed to lead his land out of chaos and injustice and play an active part in leading by example in an effort to achieve his long-term goals.

CAMELOT WISDOM:

- To answer a key question, develop an idea, or address an issue, you need a plan and a process; it's not just throwing ideas against the wall. Knowing where you want to end up—the objective—must be defined; the strategy—the theme—must link where you are to where you want to be. The tactics, mistakenly created first in many instances, come last.
- One needs to think through the potential outcomes and the potential consequences of any action. Leaders can differentiate themselves by their ability to use research and insight to make accurate predictions of possible initiatives.
- Things may start with an idea, but they should end with someone being accountable for executing the plan.
- Arthur understood the importance of communicating where you stand, simply and coherently. You need more than facts. You need an emotional connection to drive a position or program forward—the right message at the right time with the right method of delivery.
- Decisions can't be developed in a vacuum. Others affected by the decision and those who will implement it need to provide their input in order to feel an ownership stake in the decision. Otherwise, you will be faced with a lack of cohesion and commitment.
- Like Arthur, sometimes we need to make things up as we go along. Our training and our experiences prepare us to ride the unpaved roads.

CHAPTER 4

EQUAL JUSTICE: REEVALUATING AND REINNOVATING

Might for Right was a new and bold concept in Arthur's England. Yet the fact that it was new, bold, or even good was not enough for the empowered class, the nobles, to quickly adopt this important evolutionary step toward a modern society. They had very little information upon which to make a judgment. The values by which the king wanted to rule, and that he wanted his people to embrace, had no history to validate or support them.

Might for Right was a core feature of Arthur's vision for his country, but it also created a new set of questions: What is Right? What were the new benchmarks, the new values, the new rules, and how would these new values and rules be applied?

Arthur hoped to give Might for Right the teeth it needed by invigorating his armed forces with a new assignment. With the Knight's Covenant, he wanted to enforce his plan by demanding that the law be applied equally no matter what the individual's class or stature in society. This was Arthur's way of pushing responsibility and accountability down into another layer of his organization.

Compelling compliance, though, had its own set of problems. Buy-in was not and is not straightforward. Many times, our gut, our knee-jerk reaction, is to say no. It's the core of reverse psychology. Inertia or just plain pig-headedness can also thwart the adoption of a new plan. Changing lanes or getting onto an entirely new highway might be impossible if one feels locked in by pride or paranoia. And too often leaders worry first about their reputation or that their legacy might be diminished. There's always a ready excuse or rationalization.

One doesn't need to be a leader, of course, to get defensive. For gamblers, it's: "My luck would have changed if I had had one more roll of the dice (or one more card, or one more spin of the wheel)." For politicians, it's: "The media were biased or the other party was blocking our progress." In business, it's: "The marketplace wasn't ready, or the media, the analysts, had built-in biases against us."

Thus, there are usually a host of powerful reasons—political, personal, or pecuniary—to stay the course and protect the *status quo*. Circling the wagons, shielding members from attack, is the *raison d'être* of trade associations. It's not always a bad thing; some things are worth protecting. If Arthur had accepted the current norms of government, he probably would have ruled with far fewer challenges. But this is not where the story goes.

Arthur plowed new ground and knew the importance of gaining executive-level buy-in: the assent of the nobles. Without it, he had no hope of implementing the reforms. This need for bridge building and advocacy development is as important today as it was centuries ago. Few executives would venture into a boardroom with a proposal that wasn't prescreened and supported in some fashion or didn't have the backing of other top officers.

Consciously or unconsciously, conspicuously or surreptitiously, some choose to ignore or even work actively against a change. In addition, the failure to implement change could be caused by the poor qualities of the idea, a lack of good information and compelling rationale, a breakdown in communication, or a combination of these factors. The issues, the barriers, the prejudices, and the passive-aggressive behaviors—whether in full view above the table or hidden, lurking below—must be rooted out.

Speculation and surprise make the job of directing or operating in an enterprise much more difficult. Every executive I know has a "no surprises" policy (except in the case of parties, perhaps). Valuable time and energy are burned when employees speculate about the potential consequences of change and wonder who will be the winners and the losers.

The key stakeholders, no matter what the industry or sector, deserve and demand the opportunity to review and revise new ideas before being asked to endorse them. These politically astute actions call for a communications plan to provide the objectives and rationale for the proposal. From a practical standpoint, whatever you plan to do—taking things to the "next level," implementing a program, or selling a proposal—it's easier to build a broad base of support and trust when you combine facts with persuasive language to prove your points.

For all of these reasons, plans need a process of ongoing research and evaluation to help ensure that progress is being made (in the right direction, on time, and on budget). Unfortunately, generating these metrics often gets short shrift because of cost or, perhaps worse, lack of awareness and skill.

In 2008, I conducted an informal survey of the top 25 public relations agencies.[1] These companies earn billions in fees each year from companies hungry for attention, and those that sometimes want quite the opposite. I inquired if they had an in-house training program, what courses they offered, and if any were mandatory. Only eight of 25 surveys were returned; perhaps these were the firms that were most proud of their programs.

The results were still revealing. All of the respondents offered programs in the traditional areas of public relations: writing skills, presentation skills, and media relations. Some offered training in issues/risk/crisis management, advocacy/third-party relations, conflict resolution, and digital media. On the other hand, only three of the eight said that some or all classes were mandatory.

When it came to metrics and numbers, the story did not improve. Only half of those responding reported that they offered training in research methods and/or measurement, and half offered courses on budgeting and/or forecasting. It's unfortunate that numbers and words don't mix for many PR practitioners.

Again, it's back to asking questions. We need to decide, in advance of the plan's execution, which benchmarks must be achieved to stay on course, which resources should be added or subtracted, and whether or not to extend or contract the period of time needed to accomplish the objectives. Conversely, we need to know when we must modify the plan or make significant changes, or scrap the plan altogether and think anew.

> *The efforts to dig a channel for Might had failed, even when it was turned to the spirit, and now he was feeling his way towards abolishing it. He had decided not to truckle with Might any more—to cut it out, root and branch, by establishing another standard altogether. He was groping towards Right as a criterion of its own—towards Justice as an abstract thing which did not lean upon power. In a few years he would be inventing Civil Law.*
> *He was inventing Law as Power.*[2]

Over time, Arthur found that Might was not the answer. He had a bold plan, took ownership of a strategy and its implementation, but found that it was failing. He had the sense to see the flaws and began the process of moving, "groping," toward a newer, better policy.

We'd all like to get things right the first time. Though it's certainly the most desirous way of operating, it's hardly the most common. Sometimes the expedient thing, the imperfect thing, is the only thing to do. For instance, abolishing slavery at the time the United States was founded would have prevented untold suffering. The country had to wait nearly a hundred years for the Emancipation Proclamation and then another hundred for the Civil Rights Act. The sad fact, however, is that we wouldn't have the country we have today if the northern states had pushed the issue in 1776. We would not have had 13 colonies turning into 13 states. The 4th of July would have been just another day on the calendar. Whatever axiom you want to use—half a loaf is better than none or Voltaire's "The perfect is the enemy of the good" (originally, *Le mieux est l'ennemi du bien*)—incrementalism is hard to accept but equally hard to forswear.

Like the uncertainty felt by the Confederate states about their future at the conclusion of the Civil War, Arthur created a conundrum for the class of nobles in his attempt to change civilization. They weren't sure if the changes represented a threat to their positions and wealth or an opportunity to enhance them. And like all threats and opportunities, he had to deal with the rational as well as the emotional sides of the issue. Protecting self-interest, maintaining tradition, helping your fellow man, and doing what's best for the greatest number of people all had to be weighed and balanced.

Arthur had the right intention with the wrong method and he knew it. He admitted his mistake. That's the first step in re-railing a strategy: identify the strengths and weaknesses—what should be kept, what should be modified, and what should be jettisoned. Acting in the best tradition of the modern innovator and entrepreneur, he took a risk. He went forward with a plan, though there were imperfections and gaps in understanding all of the potential issues.

The trouble with this approach, however, was that it was mostly linear, heading down a path with little interruption. Plans require a regular process of reflection and reevaluation, a circular approach. Along with a continuous stream of feedback, there should be fixed points along the timeline for a review of the plan's and people's progress. Having these data aren't enough, however. The information must be converted into insights. The insights, in turn, must be converted into action. As we know, Arthur did change direction eventually. The problem was that it all took so long. In the end, Arthur would run out of time. The consequence of no or slow action may be losing the opportunity of a lifetime.

Thus, there had to be a corollary to Might for Right. In time, it would be the laws of Equal Justice that would shift the power base of leadership from the entitled elite and the military to the people. Before this new societal norm could occur, however, there were other barriers to the adoption of Equal Justice that had to be overcome, other than the lack of familiarity or a track record of positive outcomes. Beyond the cooperation of the military, Arthur could not implement his reforms unless the nobles accepted them or, at least, allowed them to exist. This was the new hurdle that Arthur had to vault. For his vision to move toward reality, Arthur needed the ascent of the titled classes, the movers and shakers of their day. In today's organization, they would be the equivalent of the board, the officers, the celebrities, and other external key opinion leaders.

Arthur needed to convince the nobility that their prospects and fortunes would grow if their people—all the people—were elevated by his new, more equitable laws. He needed to take uncertainty out of the equation and demonstrate what was in it for himself and the leadership class. Now, like then, uncertainty is a diversion that menaces management and staff alike because it leads to the incubation of rumors, an unfocused workforce, and lost productivity.

"You will find," he explained, "that when the kings are bullies who believe in force, the people are bullies too. If I don't stand for law, I won't have law among my people. And naturally I want my people to have the new law, because then they are more prosperous, and I am more prosperous in consequence."[3]

Arthur understood that keeping the populace poor, without the resources or ability to advance, was both cruel and unproductive. Equal Justice would provide the basis for allowing everyone to advance. He understood that some would challenge this notion, this new ideal; the greedy and the insecure did not want the common folk to share the wealth or own the same rights. But he didn't need everyone to agree—just enough to tip the balance, to achieve enough critical mass of opinion to begin the process of change. He had to reach out well beyond the walls of Camelot.

However, there were few methods and channels to inform and educate the dispersed nobility and populace in Arthur's day. Those that were in place were inefficient because they relied on direct contact, word of mouth, or scarce written documents. For this task of information dissemination, he developed, literally, an army of ambassadors to both spread the word and enforce the law—the Knights of the Round Table, which we'll discuss in more detail in the next chapter.

In a different time, Arthur would have been attempting to ratify a constitution, pass sweeping legislation, or sell a proposal to dramatically change the strategic direction of an organization to its board of directors. In each case, plowing new ground turns up fresh questions. People tend to see change as creating winners and losers, and in many cases that's true.

But sharing information and creating an environment of fairness creates only winners. Still, if the argument for change isn't wholly convincing, it needs only to cross a threshold that's good enough to turn opinion toward accepting a small risk in exchange for a large reward.

To the weight of opinion, Arthur was able to add two of the greatest intangibles anyone can own: trust and charisma. He knew that the adoption process had to start at the top: with him. In order to properly lay down the foundation of reform, Arthur had to be visible in his leadership by becoming the ultimate role model. He led by example and shared the glory as well as the pain. Arthur frequently joined in battles and jousts, and he understood the different classes from firsthand experience. His very character became a rallying point around which most people gathered to support his success.

> *"But all men of worship said it was merry to be under such a chieftain, that would put his person in adventure as other poor knights did."* [4]

It was important that Arthur was a sympathetic and likable person because these, at least, were characteristics people could understand. Might for Right and Equal Justice were less comprehensible, so the trust he owned automatically as king and the trust he earned as a ruler became valuable currency.

Arthur's reforms became personalized and entwined with the man. Although it was admirable that the ruler would stake his personal reputation and literally place his life on the line for Equal Justice, there are a variety of dangers to the plan's long-term success that we can see possibly emerging. Could man and ideal be separated? Could his vision succeed without him? Would the plan live on after he was no longer king?

These are some of the same issues we see with leaders and their ideas and programs today. Will the new business that was acquired become integrated and place the company on a new path, or will it be spun off to return to a previous model? Will one government change its policies on the economy, energy, health care, the environment, or funding the military only to see them dismantled in a subsequent administration? Or, are the ideas or reforms powerful enough to transcend the people and the current fashions of the day?

We should not expect that all of our plans and ideas will stand the test of time. Times change, cultures evolve, and science explains. Moving on from where we are today is necessary and inevitable. Yet, timelessness does exist. There were horrific gaps in the application of Equal Justice for all—from the peasants to the nobility—but it did endure. There were more winners than losers, and the law carried the same benefits and consequences for all the people, including the king and the queen.

Before Arthur had started his life's work, a man accusing the Queen of anything would have been executed out of hand. Now, because of his own work, he must be ready to burn his wife.

"The only way I can keep clear of force is by justice. Far from being willing to execute his enemies, a real king must be willing to execute his friends."

"And his wife?" asked Guenever.

"And his wife," he said gravely.[5]

Arthur was determined to be a role model for justice by accepting the ultimate test: his willingness to sacrifice his wife, Guinevere, and his best friend, Lancelot, if they were found guilty of the sinful and treasonous act of having an affair. Unlike some leaders we observe today who protect themselves and their friends at the expense of their constituents or their workforce, Arthur remained fair and even-handed in his judgments. In the face of true conflict and adversity, he used his power wisely and in a consistent manner. There were to be no exceptions. Even at the risk of sacrificing Guinevere and Lancelot, he had committed himself, his loved ones, and the people of his nation to the preservation of justice.

Of course, we don't need such grand ideas, visions, or plans to deserve or have fairness. All leaders and managers need to embed fairness in their business dealings and interactions, and in their relationships with customers, coworkers, and subordinates. Using power wisely, fairly, and consistently are behaviors that contribute to a healthy corporate culture, one that people want to associate with, do business with, invest in, or work for. The old adage "It's easier to catch flies with honey than with vinegar" doesn't quite capture the intent here. Being nice (or sweet) mustn't be confused with being fair. Fairness can't be a lure; it has to be a given, a value that underpins the culture—business, societal, or otherwise.

Fairness, though, is contextual. What's fair and just (or appropriate or ethical) in one time, in one place, or in one culture may be quite the foreign concept in another. Business is not democracy; it is not a place where all of its constituents get an equal vote. Nor is it always a meritocracy; the best or apparently most deserving don't always rise to the top. Indeed, I've been surprised how many times the mediocre find ways to "fall up."

"Well, Kay thinks it is unfair that you are always turning me into things and not him. I have not told him about it but I think he guesses. I think it is unfair, too."

"It is unfair." "Sometimes," he said, "life does seem to be unfair."[6]

To have any possibility of a meritocracy or to have a shot at fairness, however, a government (or any organization, for that matter) needs an educated constituency. People need to be aware, and they need to be literate so that they can take full advantage of what society has to offer. This could have been one of the key reasons why Equal Justice was not an immediate success. Arthur was concerned about everyone's welfare, but he failed to recognize the importance of education as the great equalizer. This is surprising given his own educational background. Although he wasn't a peasant, Arthur was once of lowly circumstance. His own education, as strange as it was, gave him the knowledge and experiences that helped him to think clearly, communicate with others in terms they could understand, and empathize through his sharpened perceptions.

There's always more we could have done; that's part of the process of reflecting and reevaluating. The mistake or deficiency may have been outside of our control, an oversight, or hidden in a blind spot. The process is equally important and valuable for favorable outcomes. We need to identify the areas that ought to be amplified and targeted for further refinement.

We need some introspection, too. We must be honest and fair with ourselves. Is there a nugget of truth in what others are saying? Am I in the right position? Why aren't I making any headway? You could be like Kay and complain with envy, or you could ask for what you need and want. Except for maybe a few people, we can't expect the boss to read minds. At the same time, we need to assess our own gifts and talents and understand the difference between intelligence and aptitude. Recognizing in ourselves and in others the difference between the square peg and the round hole will increase our own job satisfaction and allow us to be better career counselors for our staffs.

CAMELOT WISDOM:

- Forcing or demanding acceptance of new ideas or new values, even outstanding ones, can generate a backlash. Arthur understood that ideas and values must be embraced, not coerced. An uncertain environment breeds concern and even contempt. Unless leaders give clear direction and buy-in is achieved, valuable time and energy will be wasted on speculation, worry, and rumor generation.
- Surprises are rarely wanted or tolerated. To build support for an initiative, one must presell the concept to those who have influence over decision making and the ultimate success or failure of the endeavor.

- Arthur led by example: he held himself accountable, admitted mistakes, and moved forward. Although getting things right the first time might be ideal, we need to accept the reality of incrementalism.
- Arthur didn't know it, but a process for ongoing research and evaluation is a crucial element to any plan. Shifts in strategy, tactics, or resources are more appropriate and acceptable if they are made with the help of predetermined benchmarks.
- Facts can put you in the right, but embedding them in an emotional context can put you in the lead.
- Fairness is a concept and a practice that is greater than what is required by law or regulation. Arthur demonstrated that power and fairness are not mutually exclusive.

CHAPTER 5

CREATING A ROUND TABLE: ASSEMBLING THE RIGHT TEAM

One of the most enduring images from the court of King Arthur is the Round Table. There was both symbolism and practicality in having the knights sit in a circular pattern. Perhaps the most mentioned and commonly accepted aspect of the Table's shape was the ability of each knight to be in full view of the others. A number of modern books on communications and teamwork note that seeing who is at the Table enhances interaction and discussion. No one can hide or be forgotten, and everyone knows to whom to attribute a question or comment. It was also impossible to duck a question or a comment from a fellow knight or from the boss himself, or to get lost in the crowd when a call went out for volunteers.

The Round Table was an innovation in design, but, in terms of using resources, its manufacture was wasteful and time-consuming. Despite the beauty and simplicity of a circle, it is actually a complex task to cut wood on angles with precision and then carefully round and align the edges. Rectangular shapes are simpler and much easier to produce. But the world is not a rectangle, and it is not simple or easy. It's round like the Table.

"Also Merlin made the Round Table in tokening of roundness of the world, for by the Round Table is a world signified by right."[1]

The Round Table, a wedding gift from Guinevere's father, King Leodegrance, was a wonderful addition to Arthur's court and most assuredly broke down barriers that previously isolated some important players; the Table enhanced discussion and collaboration. Yet, its seats were not filled very frequently. The knights were on their quests, competing in tournaments, or dispersed across the country in service of the Might for Right strategy in the attempt to reach the new standard of Equal Justice.

So, with the Table empty much more often than not, why did it endure? Why did it remain a positive icon despite some of the failures in Camelot, and why is the imagery still so fresh today? From Merlin's perspective, the Table represented an ideal. Vacant or occupied, the Round Table was a symbol of what was right with the world.

The knights were human, however, and did not always remember or appreciate the higher purpose of the Table's form. They were trained as warriors. Hypercompetitiveness was rewarded. Being the "best knight" was an aspiration they all shared, but it was being the best in combat, saving the most damsels in distress, or being revered ("worshiped") by fellow knights. The best did not mean being an expert communicator, an evangelist spreading the gospel of Equal Justice.

> *"There will be a lot of jealousy," said Kay. "You will have all these knights in this order of yours saying that they are the best one, and wanting to sit at the top of the table."*
> *"Then we must have a round table, with no top."*
> *"There is room at the table for a hundred and fifty."*[2]

Arthur sat at the "top" of the Table, but it didn't have a conventional top. If it sat 150 knights, the surface area would have been thousands of square feet! Indeed, it was round, but it was in the form of a ring, allowing for people to walk across the expanse for some interchange (and for the servants to cater to the needs of the knights) without needing to walk around its lengthy circumference.

We don't know if restricting the number of knights at the Table to 150 was a physical limitation of the room in which the enormous table stood or if it was determined based upon a historical review of optimally sized organizations. The "Rule of 150," whether it started in Camelot or not, persists today. It is known that some villages, sects, and even businesses divide or bud off when the population crosses the 150 threshold. There might be a biological basis for this. Research has shown that, because of the size of our neocortex and the way the brain is wired, we don't seem able to sustain more than 150 key relationships at any one time.[3]

Andrew Cosslett, chief executive of InterContinental Hotels Group, came up with his own interpretation of the Round Table in 2005 when he formed "The Knights Group." In this case, Cosslett pulled together his top 200 managers to "gain fellowship and support and accelerate the pace of change in the company."[4] "Belonging to a group is very powerful," he noted. "We have a code and we have a language" that creates a community, a pack, that works with a common message and a common cause.

Still, Arthur's 150 was a huge and unwieldy number of day-to-day direct reports; it's too much for any one boss to manage by at least an order of magnitude. Thus, the composition of the Knights of the Round Table—their backgrounds, their skills, and their personalities—needed careful assessment. Just a few squeaky wheels could absorb a vastly disproportionate amount of the king's management time and derail days' or weeks' worth of planned activities. The team of 150 needed balance: balance in the form of staffing the Table with seasoned, worldly knights as well as young, inexperienced players filled with hope, promise, and drive.

"*. . . by mine advice ye shall choose half of the old and half of the young.*"[5]

That there should be four old and worthy knights chosen to fill four of those empty seats, and that there should be four young and ardent knights to be chosen to fill the other four seats, and in that manner all those eight seats should be filled.[6]

This staffing equation was given to Arthur by his comrade, King Pellinore: inspired advice well before the human resources function was born. (King Pellinore was also the father of several knights who joined him at the Round Table.) While we know that choosing the best team is more complicated than merely balancing the experienced with the untested, Arthur had to play the hand he was dealt, at least initially. He needed the old guard on his side. They had already proven themselves as warriors. They had a track record, a network of relationships, and a reputation. But they were the ones most likely to cling to the values of the past. The newly minted knights, without clout or reputation, were more likely to be open to his new ideas and, thus, much more supportive of the initiatives for political and social reform. So, with the rough 50:50 formula in hand, the process of populating the Table started.

It's a lesson that modern companies should heed. Circuit City, the second-largest electronics retailer in 2007, cut 3,400 of its highest-paid hourly workers as part of an effort to trim its costs. Media reports were quick to point out the impact on employee morale and the flagrant disconnect between the terminations and CEO Philip Schoonover's $8.52 million pay package from the previous year. What quickly emerged, however, were the ramifications of retaining only the less experienced sales staff. Many of the best salespeople—the ones closing the deals with customers—were gone, and a ready set of mentors vanished; as a result, revenues declined. Circuit City filed for bankruptcy in 2008 and was liquidated in 2009.

Although we don't have all the answers today when it comes to building a staff or interviewing potential recruits, there were far fewer procedures back in Arthur's day. When the sword in the stone made its appearance,

a man's lineage was about all that was required for him to take a turn at
winning Excalibur.

> . . . *very many exalted knights made application for admission, and that
> in such numbers that three heralds were kept very busy looking onto
> their pretensions unto the right of battle. For these heralds examined the
> escutcheons and the rolls of lineage of all applicants with great care and
> circumspection.*[7]

The heralds, acting as the human resources screeners, only needed
to ensure that the riffraff were kept clear. Indeed, our process of vetting
employees and political appointees still has much to be desired. Despite
the development of an unprecedented process of detailed queries by
the incoming administration of Barack Obama in 2008 (including a
seven-page survey with 63 separate requests for information), a number
of high-profile nominees went down in flames. These included former
Senator Tom Daschle for Health and Human Services secretary and
Governor Bill Richardson for commerce secretary. Either the answers to
the questions were inadequate, or the vetters themselves were inadequate,
or both.

Senator John McCain, Obama's GOP rival in the election of 2008,
chose Sarah Palin, then Alaska's governor, to be his vice presidential
nominee after a too-swift vetting process. There were serious concerns
about her readiness to be a heartbeat away from the presidency, an ethics
investigation in Alaska, her husband's DUI arrest, and her unwed teenage
daughter's pregnancy. But they communicated more. The serial revela-
tions became a reflection of the McCain team, and of the man himself
and his judgment. His reputation suffered.

Of course, this isn't new in politics. Scanning the landscape over the
last few decades, we can remember Thomas Eagleton for vice president in
1972, John Tower for secretary of defense in 1989, Zoë Baird for attorney
general in 1993, Bernard Kerik for homeland security secretary in 2004,
and Harriet Miers for the Supreme Court in 2005. The reasons for these
falls from grace are various, including mental health issues, tax problems,
outright corruption, and limited qualifications.

Asking questions is one thing, an essential thing. But equally essential is
the need to receive good answers—truthful answers—in a timely fashion. Most times, the truth will out. We can't sweep bad or embarrassing
news under the rug. It's bad for us and it's bad for business. Let's face it, our
24/7 online world is relentless in its pursuit of a good story. Someone will
always be around to ask, "What's that lump under the carpet?"

Poor vetting and oversight in the extreme resulted in the largest Ponzi scheme in history. Bernard Madoff, sentenced to a 150-year prison term in 2009, scammed his investors out of nearly $65 billion. They (and the Securities and Exchange Commission) should have asked far more questions. There are no easy answers, however, on how to overcome blind faith or greed that blinds.

Being transparent and honest is the first, best, and only approach to business, politics, and relationships. If we are to wear an ethical mantle, then we must commit to ethical standards all of the time, not just when it's easy or convenient or in public. And, we must ensure that those with whom we work or hire also adhere to those principles; employees and contractors are extensions of the organization.

It's always the case, however, that we must bend to the realities of the moment. It was no different for Arthur. The new Knights of the Round Table were, in effect, promoted quickly and far ahead of schedule. Arthur had to achieve a critical mass of manpower and needed to indoctrinate the young knights quickly before opposition could take hold.

Today we often see managers facing the dilemma of promoting employees too soon, but for a different reason. What does one do when top performers (or, sometimes, just warm bodies that might be hard to replace) are set to leave because they think they've put in the required amount of time or they've been promised promotion elsewhere? Promote them because they occupy a critical role that can't be filled in the short term? Ask for patience and push for a delay? Attempt a negotiation and offer them more money without offering the higher title? Or, do we wish them well in their new position at the other organization? Most decisions have more than one dimension or variable. The consequences of each must be assessed and weighed.

Because we work and communicate in team settings so much of the time, another consideration is the impact the itchy-to-leave employee might have on others should he or she decide to stay. People will know or guess some dealing took place, even if the incentive to stay didn't include a visible promotion, because people will talk. There may be no reaction, some may grumble and create additional distraction, and some might be emboldened to try the same tactic themselves.

Sometimes you can choose with whom to work; sometimes you can't. And some people would just like to be left to work alone. As part of an exercise in a graduate school class I taught recently, five teams of randomly assigned, similarly experienced people were set to work on comparable tasks. Most were in the same city but in remote locations and did not normally work together. After observing some struggles,

I asked each of them (about 30 people) for some feedback on how their teams were functioning and what they were doing to improve their performance. Three common themes emerged: (1) some people wouldn't do the work ("they wanted a free ride"), (2) a dictator took over the team ("before we knew it, this person was delegating"), and (3) some people would do the work if assigned but they simply would not communicate ("I sent a message and never heard back").

You may not find this example particularly unusual. Some people are passive, some are aggressive, and some are passive-aggressive. Hall of Fame baseball player and manager Casey Stengel had it right when he said, "Getting good players is one thing. The harder part is getting them to play together."

I responded to the concerns voiced by the teams with some questions: Why was it so hard to push aside individual agendas and adopt a team agenda? Did you define upfront how the team would operate? Did you discuss and agree on roles and responsibilities? Did anyone suggest a schedule or timeline? Did you discuss and agree on the best way for the group to communicate—email, IM, phone, or Facebook? If more than one person wanted to lead, did you consider rotating the position? Was time ever set aside to review and assess team performance?

After some "oh yeahs" and "we should have done thats," we discussed the importance of finding common ground, setting expectations, and keeping the focus on mutual goals. Then I made a few more queries: Why weren't these problems ever aired? Did you try to engage the individual in question? Did anyone confront the issue?

The responses were on the order of "I wanted to speak up about a problem person but wanted to avoid confrontation; I didn't want to make things worse." When I asked if there were things that held them back, I heard, "Well, I was hoping someone else on the team would step up."

> . . . it is an old saw, A good man is never in danger but when he is in the danger of a coward.[8]

We know it's hard for most people to articulate their feelings, especially around sensitive issues. Arthur, Lancelot, and Guinevere certainly knew this acutely. Few people go looking for a confrontation, but it's a critical part of working in teams, supervising others, and being a strategic adviser. But it's up to you, not someone else. And it's not "making waves." Making waves connotes stirring up trouble and creating new problems. This is about airing and addressing the issues by asking questions and seeking clarifications while showing respect for different views.

Finding the right fit for the team is a difficult task. An interview or two and calling a few self-selected references usually isn't enough to get a true sense of the candidates and how they would function in your work environment. It's imperfect, but try we must. We need to pay as much attention to knowing our own people as we do the competition. Just as we seek to understand stakeholder issues and concerns when developing a message strategy or a business deal, we need to have the same mindset when working with colleagues. Some companies use personality-screening tools and background checks, though most can't afford this kind of in-depth analysis.

The continued cohesion of a team can be helped by having at least occasional face-to-face contact. Let's take the elevator, the car, or the airplane and get back to our base, our Camelot, every now and then and sit around the Round Table for a discussion. There's the networking opportunity, of course, but face-to-face allows us to observe all the nuances and evaluate the visual cues of our colleagues. With these additional inputs, we're able to assemble a more accurate picture of strengths, weaknesses, and motivations. James Surowiecki noted in *The Wisdom of Crowds* that "a successful face-to-face group is more than just collectively intelligent. It makes everyone work harder, think smarter, and reach better conclusions than they would have on their own."[9]

In addition to dealing with the politics of teams, Arthur also had to deal with the politics of his own family. In his attempt to bring all the factions under one banner—one vision of the future—he sought a place at the Table for those who were at times disloyal or deceitful. Some of his own kin at the Table even wanted him dead. Not exactly a recipe for perfect harmony and maximal effectiveness but, again, he did what was necessary to move the country closer to his goal.

> *"It is not going badly," said the king. "You can't expect a thing like that to go smoothly the whole time. The idea is there, and people are beginning to understand it, and that is the great thing. I am sure it will work."*[10]

Arthur, in these comments to Guinevere and Lancelot, was giving a pep talk by highlighting the progress being made in converting opinions to his point of view. Conveying optimism was essential. He had to secure the perception, the firm belief that success was assured.

His was a radical plan, and it was going to take time and risk to complete. Arthur was keeping his enemies close to keep a watchful eye on their activities. He attempted to avoid surprises that could undermine or outright sabotage the plan. Yet, he also had a much less calculating reason for inclusion. It was his empathetic nature; he wanted to understand the mistrust and hate. In the days before psychotherapy, he struggled to find reason in the unreasonable and always seemed to travel much more than half the distance to find the common ground.

Finding success with a new idea can be a prolonged endeavor. Certainly, the skill and speed by which goals are achieved are some key benchmarks of leadership. However, reaching the goal is not enough to claim leadership. Leaders must re-achieve. They must continually reassert their position, continue to create relevancy, understand competitive threats, and invest the appropriate resources back into the process. Perseverance and perceptiveness can't guarantee success, but it's hard to imagine winning without them.

Commitment is crucial, and so is urgency. If you're in the process of reaching toward a goal, or if the objective has already been achieved, it's important that the sense of importance felt in the early days of the quest—even concern and worry—continue to pervade the team. There must be ongoing reminders of why we're doing what we're doing.

Unto this were all the knights sworn of the Table Round, both old and young. And every year they sworn at the high feast of Pentecost.[11]

Arthur knew that it wouldn't be good enough to set down some principles or mission/vision/values statement and hope that the political and military machinery would run on remote control. Unfortunately, many modern organizations fail to follow through on their grand gestures of creating mission/vision/values statements. Employees from different levels and functions are gathered to hammer out a document that's generic enough to apply to everyone but specific enough to embody the organization's business or sector. Yet, the work too often stops there. It doesn't go beyond a plaque in the lobby or a framed document in a conference room. There is frequently no direction on how to walk the talk.

Arthur made a formal, regular occasion of revisiting and reaffirming the mutual bonds and commitments of the Round Table. There was on ongoing opportunity to bring people together and visit with top management (the king), exchange information, and indoctrinate the new employees (the knights, partly because they were being continually killed off in wars or in battles over honor).

As we noted in Chapter Three, great prestige was attached to the Round Table. It was a privilege to serve with the king and fellow knights of such high esteem. As the renown of the knights and the Round Table grew, so did interest in joining this powerful club.

"It is strange how they come here," said his friend. "I suppose they can't keep away. Any boy with a bit of go in him feels that he has to come to Arthur's court, even if it is to work in the kitchen, because it is the centre of the new world."[12]

At Camelot, the kitchen became the ancient equivalent of the mailroom: a place to prove oneself and demonstrate a commitment to the group. Getting in was the key, the ticket to a glorious career. Today, it's like punching your ticket with an internship at P&G or a stint at McKinsey or Goldman Sachs on the way to the stratosphere of business or politics.

Arthur made a valiant effort to create the best balance of experiences, strengths, and weaknesses among his knights. Despite the careful selection of what today might be directors or vice presidents, he found a favorite. He fell victim to the common mistake of developing an overreliance on one of his knights. In this case, it was Lancelot. Lancelot turned the tide on many a battle because he was, after all, the strongest and most able of the knights (see Chapter Six). Arthur placed a lot of eggs—too many—in the Lancelot basket. When the affair with Guinevere was revealed by Mordred, Arthur's son, Lancelot was forced to flee England. With Lancelot gone, Arthur was open to attack. We can see this danger in business. Such dependence on a star player, rather than developing a stable of stars, can create a gaping hole in the organization if he or she decides to quit the rat race, leave for a better title and salary, or start a family.

For the most part, however, the Round Table created a cohesive group of energized ambassadors for change. This collective, in terms of shared training, mission, and management, fostered trust and fellowship and empowered individuals to work independently. There was fighting and there was skullduggery, but the power of the concept and the successes it managed to achieve allow us to enjoy all of the Round Table's practical and symbolic aspects today.

CAMELOT WISDOM:

- The physical construction of the Round Table represents the importance of communication and mutual understanding. Though often "on the road," the knights knew that had a common home base where they could enjoy the benefits of face-to-face interaction.
- Arthur understood the symbolism of his Table; with its cachet, it attracted the best employees of the day and fostered a sense of belonging and team spirit.

- One of the most important contributions of the Round Table didn't have anything to do with its shape—it was how people were selected to be seated. The composition of the team—valuing the old and the new employee—was what gave the Table its strength.
- No one should be made (or feel as though they are) indispensable. Overreliance on any one person can lead to a rapid unraveling of hard-won success.
- Arthur was sure to convey his personal commitment to his plan; it was important to confront issues and to display both urgency and optimism to keep his team assured and motivated.
- Achievement is not a one-time exercise. We must reassert our relevancy, and set and achieve new goals.

HOW TO BE THE BEST KNIGHT: MARRYING METHOD AND MANNER

The Knights of the Round Table shared a number of common characteristics, such as loyalty, virtue, and competitiveness. They were all encouraged and expected to reach the pinnacle, whether it was having the strongest body, standing until the end in battle, or being the most devout and holy. They wanted to be the best, not just to try their best. Although they did respect those with skills and strength superior to their own, anything less than the top was considered a failure.

There was one knight, though, who was universally considered to be the best knight in all the world: Lancelot du Lac. He was strong, skilled in horsemanship, masterful with weapons, and could almost instantly assess the weaknesses of his enemies. He had strength of body and spirit and a determination and commitment beyond all others.

It was to be the room in which this boy was to spend most of his waking hours for the next three years.
Then there were the lonely hours with poises, with many other hours out of doors—before he was even allowed to touch real arms.[1]

Like some of today's top athletes trading a "normal" childhood or adolescence in favor of an Olympic gold medal or a Super Bowl ring, Sir Lancelot's long hours of practice and apprenticeship allowed him to perfect his techniques. His was no half-way attempt; it was his life and his way of life: three years of nothing but swinging weights, swordplay, throwing spears, mock battles, riding, and learning to balance and fight with heavy armor.

Passions can also become obsessions. It's important to be aware of how your personal or professional pursuits affect your personal or professional relationships and your overall well-being. Indeed, it's important to reflect and ask What's my motivation? What's driving me so hard? It might be for more money and possessions, ego satisfaction, an endorphin high, or family pressure and expectation. At a minimum, knowing your motivating forces can help explain your behavior to yourself.

> *. . . he gave thirty-six months to another man's idea because he was in love with it.*
>
> *He wanted to be the best knight in the world, so that Arthur would love him in return, and he wanted one other thing which was still possible in those days. He wanted, through his purity and excellence, to be able to perform some ordinary miracle.*[2]

Lancelot had several forces that combined to propel him forward. In addition to love of God and country, he wanted to be the best for someone else (for Arthur's approval), for an ideal (the new civil code), and for his own sense of self-worth (by performing a miracle). No matter what was going on inside Lancelot's head, other knights far and wide wanted to be like him. Lancelot was the "rock star" of his day; he was acknowledged as the best, and his name and reputation were known all over the realm. Many adversaries simply capitulated when they found out that they had to face him. He was great.

Yet, greatness, like beauty and art, is in the eye of the beholder. People often confuse and misunderstand it. When some achieve greatness by whatever definition, it can be a letdown, intolerable, and even scary. It's the fame that frequently accompanies greatness that can lead to such feelings. Some celebrities end up hating their fame. They're disillusioned and miss their privacy. It wasn't what they thought they bargained for when they reached the top.

> *Do you think it would be fine to be the best knight in the world? Think, then, also, how you would have to defend the title. Think of the tests, such repeated, remorseless, scandal-breathing tests, which day after day would be applied to you—until the last and certain day, when you would fail.*[3]

Thus, there are consequences to being the best, so be careful what you wish for. Though some rivals did lay down their arms when they learned it would be Lancelot they would be facing, others sought the challenge. Topple Lancelot and you are automatically the best knight. Always having to prove yourself, as escape artist and magician Harry Houdini found out, may end up being fatal. Known for his ability to withstand body blows, Houdini was caught unprepared for the punches delivered by a college student, J. Gordon Whitehead. Although Houdini ignored symptoms of appendicitis for some time before, his death was likely hastened by the encounter.

For corporations, institutions, and associations, best sometimes gets confused with biggest. Of General Motor's empire in the United States, Oldsmobile, Pontiac, Saab, Saturn, and Hummer are now gone. Buick, Cadillac, Chevrolet, and GMC brands remain. As we saw in Chapter Three, there are plenty of examples where CEOs push companies together—sometimes without much in the way of complementarity—in a quest to build a bigger and bigger organization. "Mine is bigger than yours" figures prominently in these deals.

Like celebrities, there is special scrutiny, and envy and resentment, in the business world when you're number one. There's the potential for government intervention or a mandated breakup when bigness is deemed monopolistic. These actions might be inspired by federal regulators or by competitor firms trying to gain some traction by leveling the playing field. And there's the sniping and poaching that go on as one company tries to leapfrog the other. For many years, Microsoft, with its size and its computer operating system dominance, attracted the loathing of many in the technology community. As Apple passed Microsoft in market capitalization in 2010, the roles started to reverse. With iTunes, the iPhone, and iPad, Apple's increasing control and influence over how and where content is distributed may be tarnishing the famously shiny apple and inviting closer examination.

This begs the question that leaders need to ask much more often: When is big big enough? Also, how does one avoid becoming a target of frustration and anger (and scrutiny)? How does one know when one has passed the point of diminishing returns? It's part data and part judgment—reasons to have personnel assigned to keep up with the appropriate laws and regulations, and keeping the corporate ear to the rail by conducting media monitoring and market research and listening to customer feedback.

There's the question of big and big enough on the institutional scale, but we also need to ask where is good and good enough on the individual scale. Is the kind of dedication exhibited by Lancelot the best pathway to success in business, in life? Does leadership require Lancelot's single-mindedness?

Whether or not the single-minded approach is appropriate may depend on the vocation and the ultimate goal. There's no doubt that there are enough rewards out there for this type of method to ensure its continuation. There's recognition, promotion, money, and, for better or for worse, fame.

Many succeed in their endeavors, but many do not. It's a common occurrence in organizations to elevate top performers to positions of leadership. It's their pay-off for their devotion, hard work, and super-sharp skills; it's the normal track for advancement. So, why do some of these experts fail in their new roles and responsibilities? Unfortunately, being the most highly skilled or talented, or the most productive anything—lawyer, researcher, or accountant, it doesn't matter—is in no way a qualification to lead people and organizations.

It's an issue that philosopher Isaiah Berlin mused about in his essay *The Hedgehog and the Fox*.[4] Berlin expanded on one line recovered from the ancient Greek poet, Archilochus, who wrote, "The fox knows many things, but the hedgehog knows one big thing." Possessing world-class skills or knowledge is rare and wonderful. But, as discussed above, these hedgehogs may have trouble making transitions. Great institutions are hedgehogs: they know their business and their customers better than most, if not all; they have focus and determination, and are tops in their category. Whatever labels we want to assign, however, we've all seen enough examples to know that the recipes for what makes a great organization and what makes a great leader are a bit different.

Just using one ingredient for leadership may not be enough to fill the whole menu. Indeed, the hyperskilled in one area are frequently deficient in others. This may not be a problem at all; indeed, it may be a decided advantage, depending on the ultimate objective. But in the dogged pursuit of perfection, the hyperskilled likely gave short shrift to other spheres of professional and personal development.

This is a more acute problem in areas where singular efforts are the norm. Successful or high-potential workers who have distinguished themselves as individual players, or as part of small teams, can have a difficult time adjusting to a supervisory or leadership role. I have seen some brilliant scientists get promoted to managerial positions because of their technological triumphs and superior performance reviews. But then they experienced sudden and previously unknown failure. What made them a great scientist did not prepare them for leading others, making budgetary decisions, or presenting their ideas in succinct, compelling ways to the board of directors.

After the initial glow of the new recognition (and of more money) has dimmed a bit, they may feel completely ill at ease and unprepared. I have observed that when the newly anointed leaders expected to feel puffed and proud, they ended up depressed and demoralized. Some just feel overwhelmed and get ground up by their new set of responsibilities. Others seem to embrace the change.

It's hard to predict this capacity to absorb a shift in responsibilities, but it's clear that success is much more likely if there is (1) active support for the change; the professional must not be put into a sink-or-swim situation; and (2) a desire to leave one role behind for another. There are other important desires, too: the desire to do better than before, to achieve something different, to lead others to do the same, and to learn and apply that knowledge.

> *"Learn why the world wags and what wags it. That is the only thing which the mind can never exhaust, never alienate, never be tortured by, never fear or distrust, and never dream of regretting."*[5]

Continuous learning permits us to stay ahead of competitors, keeps us from getting stale, allows us to be better mentors, and makes us more interesting and relevant. Even without the desire to lead or to reach the top rung with its commitments and responsibilities, researching and developing new skills and expertise create value for oneself and one's organization.

The point was made in the last chapter that few, if any, people are truly indispensable. CEOs, presidents, generals, and clergy come and go all the time. Even companies so closely associated with their founders, such as Martha Stewart Living Omnimedia and Stew Leonard's, the world's largest dairy stores, carried on and prospered while their company's namesakes were incarcerated. That said, the more you know, the more secure you can become. There is an element of enhanced job protection as we develop a deeper knowledge base and attain a higher level of specialization. With more accomplishments, we may become more secure in ourselves and in our careers.

Arriving in this comfort zone is, well, comfortable. One can make a good living by achieving a place there. Repetition, as we know, can lead to the development of expertise, even world-class achievement. Yet, leaders don't linger in their comfort zones; they go on to develop multiple zones of comfort.

> *"Could I go out and be something, a fish or anything like that?"*
> *"You have been a fish," said Merlyn. "Nobody with any go needs to do their education twice."*[6]

Merlin scolded Arthur over his desire to repeat a lesson, not because he needed a review, but because it was comfortable. He was looking for something to do, and becoming a fish again didn't require much thought or effort. Merlin was telling Arthur to add to his knowledge base and move forward. Perfect a skill—great, but don't keep retracing your steps.

There might be any number of reasons why we hold ourselves back from venturing forward: fear, laziness, or a lack of resources. It's important to build a comfort zone, but it's crucial for leaders to go on and build another and another.

Sure, many of us would love the honor and adulation of being the best in any of our professional or personal pursuits. But, as we've discussed, this strategy for developing a more diverse array of skills is not about being the absolute best. It's about being good or great in enough categories to be a good or great leader, one who has expertise along with a powerful mission, vision, and values. One who perseveres.

The ability to sustain an effort is frequently underappreciated. Because incremental advances are hard to discern, we often see anxious leaders swapping out one set of strategies and tactics for a new set too soon; they don't allow enough time for their plans to mature. With enough patience (and resources), we know that all the baby steps can add up to become a completed marathon.

> *"You don't remember what chivalry used to be before your Arthur started the Table, so you don't know what a genius you have married."*
> *"It took him five years to set it on foot."*[7]

Trying, even if it doesn't amount to a commanding capability, counts for a lot. Trying can still bring some measure of joy and bring some valuable experience. It may also draw the attention of the organization through the demonstration of initiative. Arthur did not succeed in every endeavor. He was not the most powerful or skilled knight. He did not possess the biggest intellect. Yet, he is still remembered and still studied. His legacy remains. It's true for so many throughout history: the near-great still rate.

Trying your best, however, is frequently looked down upon as an excuse for underachievement. We live in a society where the common belief is that trying hard is for losers and that being the best is for winners. People who just try their best are often relegated to the second string, B-lists, or opening acts. But, as we know, this is not always the case.

Being the absolute best does not make us the most worthy, nor does it always translate into superiority. We're a package, a collection of strengths and weaknesses, and of insights and blind spots.

Even Lancelot, who was called the greatest knight in all the world, was one of these "packages." He had a winning personality to go along with his knightly prowess. He possessed strength, skill, and the admiration of those around him. He inspired others to move toward the goals outlined by his king. In all, his persona epitomized chivalry. He was gentle, fair, and just to the citizenry and feared by his enemies.

Unfortunately, like some of today's corporate executives, politicians, and sports stars, Lancelot was a flawed character who allowed himself to get caught up in a career-ending scandal. His affair with Guinevere undermined his friendships and his ability to lead and crushed his dream to behold the Holy Grail, for only the most pure could touch it.

So, if skills—a "good enough" mix of comfort zones—represent one side of the leadership equation, then character represents the other. Being the best means having the character to maintain and promote a sense of personal and organizational ethics, and appropriately and swiftly confront problematic issues or behaviors.

In the world of politics, we don't always elect our leaders for their intelligence or even their purity. The advantage usually goes to the one who communicates best, instills the most trust, or projects strength or character or conviction. We don't always buy the records of the best singers. Their dance moves and material (and digital reprocessing) might compensate for a voice that's good enough. The best technology may not attain the greatest market share because the company's business strategy was weak, ill timed, or undercapitalized. We may not always covet the most mechanically sound or the most efficient cars because, man, the temperamental ones look like they're doing 100 miles an hour just standing still!

Although they didn't always abide by their own ideals, Arthur and Lancelot were Camelot's role-models-in-chief. It may sound old-fashioned, but honor is never out of style. Indeed, in our increasingly suspicious and cynical society, it's an invaluable trait. The leadership (and shareholders) of today's organizations may not always act in the best manner, but they do expect good behavior of others and increasingly demand that employees sign a code of conduct and/or a sexual harassment policy. It's their attempt to set the acceptable parameters for behavior, minimize liability risks, and protect the reputation and image of the organization.

> *. . . many speak behind a man more than they will say to his face.*[8]

Employees are told how to behave, but leaders can't be followers in this regard. As leaders, we must set the tone and the limits by example, as Arthur did. We have to write, communicate, and live those principles, and ensure that they preserve and promote the organization's business through ethical behaviors. Living the code, being a role model for your organization, also means taking risks to enforce best practices.

> *. . . it is a worshipful knight's deed to help another worshipful knight when he seeth him in a great danger; for ever a worshipful man will be*

*loath to see a worshipful man shamed; and he that is of no worship, and
fareth with cowardice, never shall he show gentleness, nor no manner of
goodness where he seeth a man in any danger, for then ever will a coward
show no mercy; and always a good man will do ever to another man as he
would be done to himself.*[9]

I'm not suggesting that we put ourselves in harm's way in a physical
sense, but I do recognize that sticking your neck out in an organization in
a righteous cause can still get it cut off. Extending yourself, modeling what
"best" looks like to you and your organization, and projecting the valued
behaviors is sometimes hard and hazardous.

If others don't share your point of view, you might end up standing
alone, like the one who "volunteers" because everyone else in the line
stepped back. The fear of possible retribution for falling in with an upstart
may be overwhelming. This is something I once failed to recognize as
an unwitting maverick at a company. Rather than rally around what was
supposed to be a bulletproof proposal, people held back to see how top
management was going to react to the new initiative. It turned out that
there was more inertia for the *status quo* than I had anticipated, and I was
told by the CEO that "you can't fight City Hall." Thus, the need for some
preselling and advocacy development, as discussed in Chapter Four,
are important considerations.

If you can keep your head, though, going against the grain can be
rewarding, and taking a risk can be exhilarating. I was in an organization
that was known for being rigid: people operated from within their silos.
Some liked the little fiefdoms; they didn't want anyone to tamper with
their cliques. After setting new expectations for collaboration and business
development, however, connections with other operating units began to
flourish. Potential recruits, hearing of the new internal dynamics, started
to return phone calls. The number of proposals developed and the win rate
increased. It was a clear example of how best practices can be a business
differentiator and can enhance the organization's corporate reputation.

One can also derive a personal (even spiritual) sense of having
completed an honorable, principled activity. An accomplishment or a
victory is sweeter and the rewards can be unexpected when people are
treated fairly and with consistency. Arthur had such an experience when
he helped Robin Wood to free Friar Tuck and some laborers from the
dungeons of the treacherous Morgan le Fay. Everyone was overjoyed at
their release and offered Arthur his reward.

*"If you are going to give me a present," said the Wart slowly, "I would like
to have him. Do you think that would be right?"*

"What did you intend to do with him?

"I don't want to keep him or anything like that. You see, we have a tutor who is a magician and I thought he might be able to restore him to his wits."[10]

Young Arthur sought nothing more than to ensure the care of the disturbed Wat, one of the captives who took care of the animals at Sir Ector's estate. This is how leaders use their victories, not for the glory but for better, higher uses—to add value to the organization, the community, or the development of another individual. Good leaders, those who will last, look beyond the immediate timeframe and the immediate opportunities. Arthur may have lost some temporary treats, but he helped to rescue not just the body, but also the person. He gained an ally and the respect and loyalty that good leaders learn to recognize and nurture. From the business perspective, this type of act banks the political capital necessary to initiate new plans or initiatives that may need broad support to overcome opposition or inertia. People want to work for and rally around compassionate leaders.

Leaders and managers who adopt these behaviors on an occasional basis, however, help to create chaos, not comfort. Most people are creatures of habit and crave consistency in their lives, especially in what to expect on the job. Without that sense of continuity and comfort, the office is doomed to poor productivity from the ceaseless speculation and worry that is too often rampant at the water cooler and on the office email.

Trust and cooperation can also be eroded when some members of a management team exhibit best behaviors and others do not. The message that's received is that nice guys (or gals) finish first and so can the bad guys. This mixed message makes people wonder, "What is the incentive, then, for adopting best behaviors?" Suspicion and doubt can also linger when behaviors change after a long period of tolerating bad behavior in a management team. The questions become: What's changed? Is this the beginning of a new culture? How long will this last? and What the hell took so long?

It's important to move swiftly when correcting bad behavior or implementing a new or revised set of mission/vision/values. Without a rapid response, management and the organization will be accused of actions that were too little, too late. Being late to the game and realizing that credibility, opportunity, and loyalty have been lost can also take on a personal dimension. One faces a world of regret for not taking action when its impact would have been the most meaningful.

"They made me see that the world was beautiful if you were beautiful, and that you couldn't get unless you gave. And you had to give without wanting to get."[11]

Lancelot had this epiphany too late to realize his dream of receiving the Holy Grail. Lancelot's life, like all of ours, was full of choices. The key is to make enough good ones to minimize the guilt and disappointment.

We all have flaws, we all make mistakes, and we all make poor choices. Yet, we don't need to be right all the time or be the absolute best in all areas to win or succeed. What we do need are enough strengths—enough roundedness—to be an attractive package to move up in the organization, to lead, and to have others follow. We need the confidence to implement change, and we need to learn and develop expertise, to communicate up and down the organization, and to help others develop their potential. And part of the package also means never tolerating or rewarding bad behavior.

CAMELOT WISDOM:

- Single-mindedness (like Lancelot's) can lead to highly valued expertise in a narrow field, though good can sometimes be good enough. Arthur had a good enough intellect and good enough battle skills to move England toward his goal of unification.
- It may be antithetical to conventional wisdom, but a personal or institutional goal of being "number one" in size or scope may not always be appropriate. The time and costs involved, and the potential scrutiny that would be invited, are among the factors to be evaluated.
- Experts are often recognized and rewarded with promotions but can fail without appropriate support and continued training; to succeed in a new role, there must be a desire to create more than one comfort zone of expertise.
- Achieving new skills and mastering new information are important strategies, but there is value in making the attempt even if expertise never arrives. Incremental advances add to the sum of an individual's "package" of strengths.
- Whereas living and working honorably was a duty in Arthur's time, it is a potential business differentiator today. People want to work, support, and do business with consistently ethical organizations where the leaders set the tone for the organization.
- Swift and thoughtful action is as important to good decision making as it is to confronting bad behavior.

CHAPTER 7

PURSUING THE HOLY GRAIL: RALLYING AROUND A COMMON GOAL

In Chapters One and Four, we touched upon the importance of having a plan, whether it be for mentoring a young professional or executing a business initiative. Pursuing the "Holy Grail," however, connotes an entirely different level of effort and expected achievement. Although the Holy Grail by modern definition is something that is elusive and virtually impossible to attain, we often establish more than one set of goals for ourselves, our work, and our organizations: we look for what is attainable and we strive for something above and beyond what the averages dictate. We draw up stretch goals.

Arthur's main objective, a kingdom of peace, was his personal Holy Grail—elevating humanity by moving compassion and fairness into the mainstream. Arthur believed that his organization—in this case, England—would not reach its goal unless the energies and resources of war could be redirected to the enforcement of his vision of Equal Justice. This was his purpose in life and what he hoped would be his crowning achievement.

However, the king knew that to make this cultural transition work, he needed the agreement and outward support of influential figures. He needed to make Equal Justice the right cause at the right time. In one terrific example of business psychology, he created a celebrity culture around his support network. He cultivated and nurtured the development of an exclusive, elite force, the Knights of the Round Table, giving them the cachet and the clout to spread the new words of fairness and impose their values.

"This Round Table," said the older man slowly, "was a good thing when we thought of it. It was necessary to invent a way for the fighting men to express themselves without doing harm. I can't see how we could have done it otherwise than by starting a fashion, like children. To get them in, we had to have a gang, as kids have in schools. Then the gang had to swear a darksome oath that they would only fight for our ideas." [1]

Arthur wasn't the only one to recognize the need to create a common purpose in order to reach the desired goal, however. Agravaine and Mordred understood this when they plotted against Arthur. They couldn't overthrow the monarch by themselves, so how could they draw others into their plan?

". . . it has to be something broad and popular, which everybody could feel. . . . so that everybody can be angry."[2]

The conspirators found that emotion, not fact, was a powerful motivator. This hasn't changed. When we think about a great speech, an uplifting concert, or an inspiring teacher, we have a tough time recalling exactly what was said, heard, or taught. But we know how we felt.

Anger, as Agravaine and Mordred knew, can trump the other emotions. It's the common glue of protest and of revolution. In the United States, Republicans seem to understand this better than Democrats. The Democrats may have a big advantage in the humor department (as the successes of the *Daily Show* and the *Colbert Report* on cable TV's Comedy Central can attest), but the Republicans have the edge in harnessing fear and anger. They know that positioning an issue as something that is being taken away from citizens evokes a much stronger, energizing (or sometimes inflammatory) response than adding to what we already have. For some, the benefit of adding health care coverage for more Americans was blotted out by the perceived threat of taking away the choice of having benefits or not. Efforts to trace ammunition and limit the sale of assault-type weapons are, again, a perceived threat to personal liberty or constitutional rights. The campaign theme "Take Our Country Back" encapsulates the message strategy.

Perception is what counts; it's how we see our own reality. Facts are supposed to inform our choices and support our points of view. People can recite the dangers of smoking cigarettes, overeating, abusing drugs, or riding without a motorcycle or bicycle helmet, yet millions ignore the facts.

There are other circumstances where people just refuse to acknowledge a fact as fact. Have you noticed that some arguments are never won despite having solid, unassailable information? If the facts don't fit the person's worldview or "frame," as University of California, Berkeley, cognitive linguist George Lakoff terms it, they bounce off like bullets shot at Superman's chest. Your opponent deflects all the data while you get blue in the face.

Certainly there are internal and external forces at play. There may be inertia: "That's the way we've always done things." There may be no consequences: "Who's going to notice, who's going to care?" We may feel powerless: "I don't have the resources, I don't have the access." Still, we pump out what we think are compelling facts in the hope of persuading people to take some sort of desired action.

But if facts were all that mattered, we'd be done. Insight alone does not produce change. Those who came after Freud quickly discovered this truism. Indeed, a whole new genre of psychotherapy (i.e., cognitive therapy) came to life based on the knowledge that knowledge doesn't bring change. It's the desire to change that brings change.

Interest in change and great ideas, even those powered by anger, can run out of steam. There is no guarantee that what is fashionable at the moment will become policy or get woven into a new societal norm. You or the idea or both can, for a million reasons, fall out of favor. Indeed, experience shows us that people are quick to claim ownership (or at least a stake) in the idea when things go well and are just as quick to desert when the first smell of defeat hits the air.

The steam ran out for Arthur and his strategy of Might for Right, too. Certainly, those out of power or who perceived a diminution of their influence continued to oppose change. But that's a problem for any age. The issue here was more of old dogs and new tricks: the knights weren't able to keep their high purpose for long. They soon relapsed into their old, war-gaming ways.

> *"But it has turned into sportsmanship."*
>
> *"All these knights now are making a fetish of it. They are turning it into a competitive thing."*
>
> *"Everyone gossips and nags and hints and speculates about who unseated whom last, and who has rescued the most virgins, and who is the best knight of the Table."*[3]

Arthur put an incredible experiment in motion, a bold move to replace old with new, to strangle anarchy and imbue civility. Infighting began to infiltrate Arthur's new order; competitiveness started to undermine any gains. There were warning signs that he needed to intervene, but Might for Right started to degenerate into just plain old Might. Even though Arthur had to suffer with a primitive communications network, there would have been enough interaction and word-of-mouth for him to have realized that he was being too hands-off.

> *"We have achieved what we are fighting for, and now we still have the fighting on our hands. Don't you see what has happened? We have run out of things to fight for, so all the fighters of the Table are going to rot."*

"I ought to have rooted Might out all together, instead of trying to adapt it."[4]

Why don't we pay closer attention to the warning signs of discontent or react sooner when a plan is clearly going off the rails? Poor listening and observational skills or a fear to act could be some possible explanations. Or, it could be that we're overly sensitive to being labeled a "micromanager." Finding the right balance between getting involved and allowing local control can be hard. Leaders need to assess the skills and experience of their group, and have open communications where expectations and management style can be discussed. Creating too much distance, a common tactic to overcompensate for either the impulse or implication of being a micromanager, will create the gaps into which good intentions can fall.

Creating a gap, whether intentional or not, is just one form of disengagement. Leaders can get distracted by any number of internal or external activities, personal or professional. A lack of patience, poor follow-through, or a case of attention-deficit disorder where a leader has moved on to the next business idea or leadership fad could end up leaving to other managers who may not have the appropriate training or background to properly finish the job.

Another common, unrealistic expectation that leaders have is that their wishes or commands will be carried forward in a more or less precise manner, and with the same level of passion and commitment. No one will know just how important an issue is or how truly committed you are to a goal unless it is communicated. People are not mind readers. You should never say to yourself, "Gee, I wish they asked me about this before it all fell apart." It's the job of the leader to be in front of the problems, not behind.

So, while recidivism may explain part of what went wrong with the Round Table, there were deeper, more fundamental issues at play. Arthur's strategy to reach his Holy Grail, it turns out, was based on a flawed foundation.

"When I started the Table, it was to stop anarchy. It was a channel for brute force, so that the people who had to use force could be made to do it in a useful way. But the whole thing was a mistake. No, don't interrupt me. It was a mistake because the Table itself was founded on force. Right must be established by right: it can't be established by Force Majeur."[5]

Arthur followed now well-established business principles in developing his plan for England. But he also fell into a common trap: he didn't adequately vet his strategic and tactical plan. There was no research or analysis, no reality check, no discussion about how the scenario might unfold, and no real opportunity to gather input from others. Merlin, his closest adviser, was of little use because he already knew (having already lived the future) that Arthur's reign would come to a tragic end. Destiny couldn't be avoided. (We'll address the issue of destiny in more depth in Chapter Fourteen.)

If force was the element that Arthur wanted to eliminate as a weapon for subjugating people, force could not be the stick to modernize the culture. Arthur recognized this, but well after his plans were in motion. After analyzing his mistake, Arthur concluded that he needed a new initiative, a tactical shift to reenergize and rebuild support.

> *"Merlyn," he said, "approved of the Round Table. Evidently, it was a good thing at the time. It must have been a step. Now we must think of making the next one."*[6]

The next big idea was literally to find the Holy Grail. Realizing that he would not be able to quell the rumblings in his court by his say-so alone, Arthur captured the imagination and commitment of the knights and kings by invoking a higher authority: he set them out on a mission from God. Unfortunately, he again failed to think this course through to its logical conclusion. The vast majority of those on the quest were too imperfect to get close to the Grail, so this new effort also turned out to be a temporary fix.

> *So he had sought for a new channel, had sent them out on God's business, searching for the Holy Grail. That too had been a failure, because those who had achieved the Quest had become perfect and been lost to the world, while those who had failed in it had soon returned no better.*[7]

After having some eggs broken in one basket, Arthur placed them into another only to find, again, a batch of shattered shells and oozing yolks. There is seldom one solution to complex problems, especially an undertaking as complicated as a cultural transformation. Even great ideas will not solve all the problems associated with a multifactoral issue. Rather than "one size fits all," one needs to think about several potential solutions to be implemented in succession or in combination.

Many executives and founders of companies have gotten to the top by making a great leap: "the big idea." But they sometimes flame out, not really having the temperament or skills for executive management. In some cases, there's recognition that the baton must be passed to another with more suitable skills and experience. Twitter's co-founder and CEO, Evan Williams, took a voluntary demotion in late 2010 to focus on product strategy but remains on the board. COO Dick Costolo moved to the top spot.

But it's common to see founding executives get too entrenched in making the big idea work at all costs or drawing out the idea in nearly endless variations to sustain power and prestige. They treat their Holy Grail as a bit too, well, holy—immutable, untouchable. An example is the well-known "founder effect": being too isolated, being too enamored with one idea or one way of thinking, and not knowing when to step aside for new or different leadership. Not only was Arthur the founder of the new vision for England, he was also the king. Thus, there were two elements stacked against creating an environment where people were free to exchange ideas and challenge the thinking of the CEO.

Though the quest for the Holy Grail was not the best way to create a common purpose, Arthur was on the right track. Rallying around an appropriate goal is one part of it. The other is getting people to rally around each other. Identifying and achieving a common purpose can be facilitated by first finding the common ground. Disparate groups or individuals can be brought together to create a common experience.

This very strategy was used in 1995 to help unify South Africa. This Holy Grail wasn't a spiritual pursuit, however. It was a rugby championship. As South Africa was set to host the 1995 Rugby World Cup, President Nelson Mandela sought an improbable goal: inspire the country and decrease racial tensions and prejudice by getting to the final match and upsetting the odds-on favorite from New Zealand.

In 1994, the newly elected president hoped that if a mostly black nation could embrace a mostly white team, the stubborn remnants of apartheid might be pealed away. As chronicled in *Playing the Enemy: Nelson Mandela and the Game That Changed a Nation* by John Carlin (and later in the 2009 movie *Invictus*), Mandela did not take the obvious route. Rather than banish the name and colors associated with the Springboks rugby team in the time of apartheid and starting anew, he embraced them. He was one with them and he invited others to join in support.

The common ground and common purpose can be found in the pursuit of an object, a policy, or a business deal. They're all goals to reach. People can also be drawn together by common experiences. It explains the growth of groups like Outward Bound, with about 40 schools around the world that "turn individuals into high-performance teams and leaders."

Wat (mentioned in Chapter Six) and the Dog Boy were not likely subjects to find a common bond. Wat, who was without a nose, bit off the nose of a child (Dog Boy) after being harassed and pelted with stones. Dog Boy was in charge of the kennels at Sir Ector's when he and Wat were kidnapped by Morgan le Fay.

> *"On the morrow Wat and the Dog Boy were the firmest of friends. Their common experiences of being stoned by the mob and then tied to columns of pork by Morgan le Fay served as a bond and a topic of reminiscence, as they lay among the dogs at night, for the rest of their lives."*[8]

No, I am not advocating stoning or bondage. Nor am I suggesting what seems to have become the standard, quick, and easy solution to generate some employee bonding: the company-sponsored happy hour. Sorry to disappoint, but sharing an experience that ultimately enhances the organization involves more than cheap wine and microwaved hors d'oeuvres. While having a party is nice (maybe even fun if it's not so forced that it's become a dreaded affair), it's not the responsibility of the organization to show you a good time. It needs to support you so you can support it. A project, an assignment, or a course or training exercise (maybe with a happy hour thrown in!) are more appropriate ways to encourage camaraderie with a purpose.

The Holy Grails we pursue today don't need to be grand (or holy). We all have ambitions, small and large; we don't need to be thinking about "swinging for the fences" every time we set a new goal. Some may qualify as a personal or professional Holy Grail. But, whatever the goal, we need to recognize that we need a plan: How will it get done? What resources are needed? Who needs to be involved? How much time will be needed to reach the goal? How will we measure our success?

Perhaps the plan will be hatched with the assistance of a mentor or a team of colleagues, but, in any case, big plans require research, discussion, buy-in from other influencers and decision makers, and follow-through. We must recognize that mistakes will be made along the way, and we should be prepared to fine-tune the approach(es) in midstream. Depending on the events and conditions, we may even need to halt, full stop, and rethink and relaunch the quest.

CAMELOT WISDOM:

- Arthur hoped to use a common purpose and a common bond—the quest for the Holy Grail—to channel the energies of his knights, but temporary fixes may end up causing more grief and harm. To reach our goals, we need the right cause at the right time.

- Leaders put plans in motion but then can't operate by remote control. Arthur needed to pay closer attention to missed opportunities, the quality of his team's work, and the warning signs of a plan going wrong.
- No one, not even Merlin, can read minds. You must clearly communicate your needs and intentions; otherwise, there will be disappointment that goals weren't pursued with your passion or commitment.
- Creating a position or a plan using facts alone may not always make a convincing case. Arthur's adversaries knew that the most powerful arguments inject emotions that resonate with their audience.
- Insight alone doesn't produce change; it's the desire to change that brings change.
- It's laudable to set high targets or big goals. But "Holy Grails" can end up being a disappointment if they're unrealistic. Less grand but still important steps might be more appropriate. And, when linked together, you may well end up with the chalice.

CHAPTER 8

PICKING YOUR BATTLES: NAVIGATING THROUGH YOUR AUDIENCE AND ENVIRONMENT

We're all familiar with the rhyme "For he who fights and runs away / May live to fight another day; But he who is in battle slain / Can never rise to fight again." Oliver Goldsmith's 18th-century sentiment has helped to forge the common sense wisdom of knowing which battles to fight and, if indeed there is a battle that must be fought, when to launch the assault. There are many examples, however, of battle-picking much earlier in time—how to do it effectively as well as the consequences of ignoring the battle—in the stories about King Arthur and his court.

In its simplest interpretation, picking your battles has been translated into "tomorrow is another day." This is driven, in part, by the most basic of instincts: the very rational, primal need for self-preservation. In other regions of our brains, however, there are other drivers of our decisions: the urgent needs to satisfy the ego, to exact revenge, and to obtain pleasure. However, to hold on to hope, and sometimes our sanity, we must be able to deny certain truths or inevitabilities. We have a difficult time admitting defeat, and we can't afford to allow the troops (or any subordinate) to see us in an inferior position. The consequences could be damaging to the soul as well as to our future ability to persuade, negotiate, and lead.

> "My fair fellows, be not dismayed, howbeit ye have lost the field this day. And many were hurt and sore wounded, and many were whole. My fellows, said King Arthur, look that ye be of good cheer, for to-morn I will be in the field with you and revenge you of your enemies."[1]

The ability to read the enemy and make strategic decisions in the heat of the moment enables commanders to preserve the necessary troops and material to either dig in to defend a position or retreat, regroup, and go on the offensive. Just like military officers, executives must survey the business terrain, assess the strength of their opponents and their chances of victory with the equipment and people at hand, and determine what additional resources might be needed.

Obviously, reading a situation in a fast-moving environment, or as a situation takes on a swelling seriousness, requires a keen eye, calm nerves, and more. We need facts and, if possible, trusted people to help us collect solid intelligence and analyze it in an objective way. Precision is better than blunt or random force. We want to target our effort, limit collateral damage, and avoid creating unintended consequences.

> *"But when men be hot in the deeds of arms oft they will hurt their friends as well as their foes."*[2]

The size, type, and proportion of an offensive move or a defensive response depend on the current circumstances and potential future conditions. Without the ability to do this on our own or with a team, one could very easily under- or overcorrect an issue. Beyond the possibility of doing more harm than good, resources may be wasted, opportunities may be lost, and credibility may be undermined.

> *The jouster had to find out the greatest length which he could manage with the greatest speed, and he had to stick to that. Sir Lancelot . . . had several sizes of spears and would call for his Great Spear or his Lesser Spear as occasion demanded.*[3]

A failure to properly assess and address the destruction of the Deepwater Horizon drilling platform, the horrific loss of 11 lives, and the catastrophic release of oil into the Gulf of Mexico in 2010 led to the ouster of BP chief executive Tony Hayward. He possessed the intellect but not the emotional intelligence required to lead the response to the crisis. In addition to the size and type of the efforts he engineered and led, his tone in words and his actions were also terribly out of alignment with the public, political, and environmental needs. *The Wall Street Journal* reported, "By most accounts, it was Mr. Hayward's inability to generate much empathy from the U.S. public that led to calls for his ouster."[4]

But it went beyond his well-reported gaffes (the most egregious of which were attending a yacht race in England while the Gulf habitat and economy suffered, and when he said flippantly, "I'd like my life back"). It was his failure to understand and relate; he didn't grasp (or, perhaps, want to acknowledge) how large and serious the spill was, and he was unable to sustain a heartfelt connection with his key stakeholders. Unfortunately, he wasn't the only casualty in this battle; the Gulf and its people will take years to recover.

In the battle for political power, Democrats lost control of the U.S. House of Representatives in the 2010 midterm elections in dramatic fashion—the highest net loss for a political party since 1948. President Obama took responsibility for this "shellacking," saying, "We were so busy and so focused on getting a bunch of stuff done that we stopped paying attention to the fact that leadership isn't just legislation. That it's a matter of persuading people. And giving them confidence and bringing them together." This revelation came too late for Mr. Obama and not at all for Mr. Hayward.

Battles, of course, can take the form of any type of confrontation—a simple argument, a personal attack, a political demonstration, a board-room dispute, a tough negotiation, or a business boycott. A battle can erupt even when trying to initiate a discussion or a relationship with a reluctant other. Indeed, the consequence of attempting to force the development of a relationship or rushing past the milestones of familiarity, confidence, and trust is that it can leave us in a weaker position. One's true intentions can be debated and viewed with suspicion. Questions come flooding to mind: Why now? Why not before? Why me? What's in it for you? What's in it for me?

Merlin taught Arthur early in his tutelage to take that important "step back" from a situation. It's important to understand the correct time course of events for relationship building: knowing when to speed things up and when to slow things down. It boils down to the critical element of knowing your audience.

"Let him alone," said Merlyn. "Perhaps he does not want to be friends with you until he knows what you are like."[5]

Pushing yourself onto another (in this case, the initial attempt to befriend Merlin's owl Archimedes) might be an innocent expression of interest. Or, it might be a calculated move. The hurried friendships—the forced and false intimacy—we see frequently in business, especially in those attempting to sell a product or a service, might be welcomed by some but repugnant to others. I'll admit, it bothers me to be called "friend" by someone I just met, especially if I see that some sort of pitch is on the way. Unless it's a case of "love at first sight," relationships must be allowed to develop.

Knowing how to build relationships—reading the verbal and nonverbal signs, learning as much as you can about your audience—is also about knowing the right time and place to raise issues and make comments. Choosing the right time to speak—when to keep things upbeat or when to go negative—is the next level of understanding how to build and navigate relationships.

Saying the wrong thing can be excused if it's an unusual occurrence and your reputation allows you to receive the benefit of the doubt. Sir Kay, Arthur's foster brother, was sometimes quite boastful, an opportunist who claimed credit for deeds half-done or not done at all. He viewed his reputation as something he was entitled to, not something he needed to earn. He could be excused, somewhat, for being young and jealous, for he saw Arthur, with his kind and unassuming nature, being embraced by his own "real" family. His cockiness earned Kay a warning from Merlin about how and when to use his mouth, an earlier equivalent of telling someone to "put your mind in motion before you put your tongue in gear."

> ". . . thou wast ever a proud and ill-tongued speaker, and a misfortunate one. Thy sorrow will come from thine own mouth."[6]

Picking your battles, as we covered earlier, is as much about knowing when to advance as when to retreat. This is the give-and-take of negotiation in business: contracts, acquisitions, mergers, and raises and promotions. Knowing the inflection point of diminishing returns, or the point where additional efforts have the opposite of the intended effect, is both an analytical skill and an art of interpreting behavior.

> And some of these high and mighty lords were filled with anger and indignation that they had not succeeded, and others were ashamed that they had failed in that undertaking before the eyes of all those who looked upon them. But whether they were angry or whether they were ashamed it in no wise helped their case.[7]

One can try, try again, and try for a third time, but you need to know when to move on. Arthur pulled the sword from the stone; he fulfilled the criterion, which was publicly available knowledge, for becoming king. It was a waste of time and emotional energy to deny the truth, the destiny of his ascendancy to the throne of England.

Sometimes the need to move on is hard to recognize. In relationships, you might be viewed as not being able to "take the hint" or, in the extreme, of being a stalker. You might have been told that you were "too close" to an idea or "too much in love" to let go. Without some insight and perspective, though, you'll be accused of stubbornness or being tone deaf to the needs and interests of the organization, another person or a client. That happened to me once. I was convinced that a client was doing a disservice to herself and her firm by ignoring a "golden opportunity" to be the first to enter a new market segment. I should have kept to my own "three strikes and you're out" rule, but I tried a fourth time and, instead of getting a grateful reaction for being persistent and passionate, I got a rebuke.

Just how far to push is the job of the negotiator. The best ones know just how far to go in order to secure the best deal possible. The most successful activists can effectively gain awareness (and funding) for their causes for the same reasons. They can gauge just how far to agitate before the sympathies of public opinion begin to turn against them; many a planned boycott or protest has been called off or curtailed for just these reasons.

> "... but an thou tarry on them any longer, thy fortune will turn and they shall increase. And therefore withdraw you unto your lodging, and rest you as soon as ye may, and reward your good knights with gold and with silver, for they have deserved it."[8]

This was a lesson that Merlin imparted to Arthur at the end of the famous Battle with the 11 Kings (including King Lot, the father of Agravaine, Gaheris, Gareth, and Gawaine) at Bedegraine. Merlin knew that, despite great success, the opposing kings would not be toppled—that day, at least. Moreover, he knew that other enemies of the 11 Kings were poised to finish the job.

Arthur's choice was to stop the battle and leave the enemy weakened, in disarray and open to attack by other enemies, or to carry on, lose more men and material, and risk creating much deeper feelings of hate toward the victor. Hate, as we all know, can be a force that's powerful and difficult to control. Like fire, it can be destructive or it can be put to good use. Sometimes we've seen hate (and in its lesser form, anger, as we discussed in Chapter Seven) in the role of ally—an energizer, the "twelfth man on the field." In the extreme, it is a rallying point that can help to create, attract, and unleash fanatics who feel, correctly, that they have little to lose by engaging in vicious, go-for-broke attacks.

Knowing just how far to push before the tide turns has a less confrontational corollary: knowing when to agree to disagree. When two opposing knights (Sir Lamorak and Sir Meliagrance) were ready to kill each other in a dispute over which of their queens (Guinevere and Morgause) was most fair, one drew back. Lamorak, a trusted soldier in Arthur's cause, knew that men had died for less, but, in this new culture that he was helping to build, such disagreements had to have a more favorable outcome than leaving blood on the battlefield.

> *"I am loath to have ado with you in this quarrel, for every man thinketh his own lady fairest."*[9]

Of course, we have our own beliefs—sometimes strong ones, passionate ones. We have our own way of looking at the world, our opinions on whom we want to support and those whom we don't, and our own strategies on how we take on important assignments. Taking that step back or that deep breath, and gaining some perspective and perhaps demonstrating a bit of tolerance, are crucial measures to gain calm while under fire. Of course, no one can tell you not to be stressed. We can't turn things like this on and off like a light switch. If you are unable to gain control under stressful circumstances, it might help to have an organizational environment that provides some resources to help you recognize when control might be slipping away, and where trusted colleagues or staff might be relied upon to give a figurative (or literal) kick under the table.

There is yet one more way to view picking your battles. Moving beyond agreeing to disagree, opposing sides can find the common ground, identify what matters most, and join forces, combining resources to look for the win-win. This is collaboration versus competition.

Another knight of some renown, Sir Tristram, interrupted a battle when he saw the courage and conviction displayed by a rival faction led by the king with the hundred knights. Clearly, in the warfare of business, this is an unlikely prospect. The point is that there are opportunities to put aside differences that would otherwise lead to a fight and instead negotiate or bargain for the common good.

> *". . . now I see your courage and courtesy I will withdraw my knights for your pleasure, for evermore a good knight will favour another, and like will draw to like."*[10]

In the opposite direction from actively choosing a course of action, there is action by default—the pocket veto of decision making. Indecision, of course, is a decision for remaining on course, even if that course means heading straight for a cliff. Decision paralysis can occur (much to the frustration of others) when legitimate choices are in view. Sometimes, however, we choose to keep our choices out of view, away from our consciousness. There is a real seduction in just not wanting to know. We all, at some point, have found refuge and peace of mind in ignorance. Not wanting to know can help us maintain our mental health because it creates some deniability: the truth can sometimes be too painful. This is why it is said that "ignorance is bliss."

Avoiding the realities of hard problems or uncomfortable situations, however, is not a leadership quality. Indeed, avoidance behaviors can have catastrophic consequences. Lancelot ignored the obvious consequences of sleeping with the wife of his friend and ruler. In addition to the affair, among the numerous issues Arthur ignored for much too long were the failure of Might for Right and the restlessness of some of his knights, the signs that his own son had nefarious intentions, and the bad blood with the Cornwall clan—his half-sisters who blamed him for his father's transgressions. King Pellinore added to the mess when he killed King Lot and, in return, Lot's sons killed several of Pellinore's children.

> *Suspicion and rumour and counter-recrimination had obscured the issue almost before it started. The Pellinore feud, the old Pendragon-Cornwall feud, the Lancelot entanglement . . . all these mixed themselves together into a fume of venom which coiled about the Queen.*[11]

Falsely accused of attempting to poison Gawaine (When, in fact, she was trying to mend fences), Guinevere found herself with few who would believe her. The long-standing misunderstandings and conflicts were taken as evidence against the queen. If divisions, feuds, and rumors are not addressed in a timely way, the organization and its people will surely suffer.

The dot.com bust at the turn of this century provides a host of examples of this failure to confront. In Europe, there was the spectacular collapse of Boo.com in 2000, a sports and high-fashion "e-tailer" that was called the next amazon.com. Investors in the venture included Bernard Arnault, the chairman of luxury group LVMH, investment bank J. P. Morgan, and a fund backed by Lebanon's powerful and wealthy Hariri family. Aside from the excesses of lavish parties and air travel by the supersonic Concorde, Boo.com's principals failed to act in time to scale back their ambitions from overly optimistic and unfounded forecasts. This lack of rigor, experience, and market intelligence allowed the company to burn through all its cash—$130 million—and no additional funding was forthcoming.

On the other side of the Atlantic, Webvan, the online grocery business, had a high-profile meltdown in 2001. Cofounded by Louis Borders of Borders Books fame, and with other backers including Benchmark Capital, SoftBank, and Sequoia Capital, it raised well in excess of $1 billion in private and public money. The beginning of the end started with a much-heralded merger with HomeGrocer.com, a conversion of those sites to Webvan technology, and a "build it big, build it fast" program of infrastructure development. Unfortunately, the rapid push for integration did not go smoothly, and, without adequate outreach and education of its customer base, online ordering dropped sharply. Cash disappeared when the rush to build a billion dollar's worth of high-tech warehouses far outstripped revenues of less than $200 million in 2000.

Their inexperience merged with their hubris to create classic founder effects: the lack of self-reflection and objectivity. The behavior is a bit reminiscent of the teenage years: "No one understands it as well as I do," "It's someone else's fault," and "Don't blame me!" Indeed, both of these young dot.com companies complained that negative press reports were at least partly responsible for their demise.

But failures certainly aren't confined to immature, untested companies. Some venerable institutions have also succumbed to these kinds of breaks from reality. In a series of complex and interwoven schemes, not one but two industry giants endured a massive implosion in the early 2000s. Enron, one of the world's largest energy companies with about 21,000 employees, and its Big Five accounting firm, Arthur Andersen, with about 85,000 employees, are all but gone now. Enron investors, including its employees' retirement plans, lost $60 billion. There were a host of indictments and criminal convictions and even a suicide as a result. In addition, Enron contributed to the drastically higher energy prices, energy shortages, and rolling blackouts in California that played a role in the eventual recall of Governor Gray Davis in 2003.

As Enron began to unravel, appearances were kept up with positive conference calls and substantial donations to charitable organizations. The company even had built a sham trading room at its Houston headquarters to impress Wall Street analysts. Executives were manipulating people, manipulating the energy market, and manipulating the books. What they couldn't manipulate, they tried to cover up. And like the dot.com companies that went bust, Enron blamed negative publicity for eroding investor confidence.

For Arthur, attempting to maintain appearances of happiness and harmony within Camelot eventually led to his demise. Avoiding a confrontation with Guinevere and Lancelot provided his son, Mordred, with an opportunity to expose the affair and humiliate the king. You're living in a fantasy world if you believe in your own invulnerability or that something can't happen because it hasn't happened already. Perhaps for these reasons, or maybe because he didn't want to confront the loss of his best friend, Arthur reassured Lancelot that a coup would never happen.

> *"You are imagining things," he announced. "Go home to bed, my friend, and forget it."*
> *". . . the situation is imaginary."*[12]

Refusing to take advice or believe that he could be undone, Arthur was left in a vulnerable state. Mordred and Agravaine were able to expose the affair, prove the betrayal, and develop new allies. From then on, the king was preoccupied with piecing the fragments of his life back together again.

Just think about how many corporate failures and shareholder suits could have been avoided if corporate leaders had only removed their heads from the sand and acknowledged reality. Unfortunately, the list of companies that have crashed on the rocks for this very reason continues to grow.

It was delay in confronting the wickedness in his own son, however, that caused Arthur's death. An older Arthur was able to kill Mordred, but not before he was struck with a mortal wound. If Arthur had picked different battles, we would have seen less bloodshed, less division, more trust, and a more rapid adoption of his plan for the future.

CAMELOT WISDOM:

- Success rarely follows a straight line upward. When things went astray, Arthur never blamed others for his failings.
- Arthur's achievements in battle were linked to his ability to gather and read his enemy's signals and make quick and calm strategic decisions—retreat, regroup, or reload—in the heat of the moment.
- Time must be reserved for building authentic relationships inside and outside the organization; the insights, mutual understanding, and trust gained are incalculable.
- Reputation is not something that one is entitled to; it must be earned. Past deeds can buy you time or the benefit of the doubt, but that well can be emptied in very short order.
- Arthur knew just how hard to push his people and his adversaries. Knowing the inflection point of diminishing returns is both an analytical skill and an art of interpreting audience behavior.

- The values of Equal Justice helped to create a more civilized, humane environment that allowed for differences to be settled, or at least tabled, by agreeing to disagree.
- While denying reality may sometimes be required to maintain sanity, Arthur found that avoiding the truth can destroy the best-laid plans, and even have deadly consequences.

CHAPTER 9

WHEN OTHERS USE CANNON: EXPECTING THE UNEXPECTED

In the last chapter, we discussed picking your battles in terms of strategy: what to look for, how to keep perspective, and when to move ahead or retreat. The keys to success in battle-picking are to have keen observational skills, to be able to analyze and synthesize information quickly, and to be surrounded by a trusted cadre of colleagues who are strong and expert enough to provide perspective and balance. But what happens when the information is tainted? How do you deal with propaganda or when others play dirty?

The rule here is not to be surprised at the tactics of others. One can be saddened, but not surprised, that some people will not have your ethics or sense of fair play. The Bible is full of deceptions, be it the trickery by Jacob to receive the blessings and birthright from his father, Isaac, which should have been bestowed on Esau, or the plot by Joseph's brothers to sell him into slavery because of their jealousies. People have always been treacherous. People have always spread rumors. People have always flaunted the rules.

> "... Mordred is using guns."
> Rochester asked in bewilderment: "Guns?"
> It was too much for the old priest's intellects.
> "Now that the guns have come," said Arthur, "the Table is over."
> "To use cannon against men!"[1]

Arthur and the bishop (Rochester) were astounded, angry, and infuriated at Mordred's use of cannon. Those were the terror weapons of the day, weapons so powerful that no "normal" mind could have contemplated using them against fellow men. Today, the use of cannon evokes images of primitive battles fought long ago—heavy balls lobbed at the enemy without warheads, or the use of targeting lasers or global-positioning satellites. Despite the success that German U-boats had in sinking ships carrying millions of tons of supplies headed to England during World War I, the British considered submarine warfare ungentlemanly. The rules of acceptability are changing all the time in war and in society at large.

Change can take us in a new direction or, upon deep reflection or after committing a serious mistake, back to an earlier position. And, in a society as diverse as ours, changes can leave us in conflict. Just look at how American society supports a growing, multibillion-dollar pornography industry while wide swaths of cultural sentiment get more and more conservative.

What passes for normal can be adopted very gradually or with a surprising jolt. The slow evolution from the general store to grocery store to the supermarket to the mega-box warehouses has led us to expect more and more choice with less and less travel. This one-stop shopping phenomenon also makes mega-malls and Internet shopping so popular. On the other end of this normalcy trajectory, we see airport screeners and searches as a rather sudden fact of life following the terror attacks on September 11, 2001.

The redefinition of a new normal is usually borne out of necessity or crisis. Arthur hoped Equal Justice would be a new normal after wars and infighting threatened the kingdom. In the pivotal battle of Bedegraine, however, we see Arthur with a different kind of need. King Lot was poised to crush his rival and, with him, hopes for unification and a more civil England. Arthur was "wildly outmatched" three to one and needed either a way out or a way to win in a hurry.

Instead, he attacked by night. In the darkness, with a war-whoop—deplorable and ungentlemanly tactics—he fell on the insurgent camp.[2]

Arthur tossed aside the established etiquette of gentlemanly, open warfare in his desperation to win and to survive. In this particular jolt to normalcy, he shifted the parameters of war with the audacious move of bypassing the front lines of sacrificial serfs and going straight to the heart of the leadership, which was nestled in what was supposed to be a secure position. Arthur's enemies, the 11 Kings (including King Lot), were completely bewildered, as were their armies. They lost the battle while they were attempting to comprehend the strange behavior of Arthur and his allies (Kings Bors and Ban). Moving forward in time, guerilla warfare, the sneak attack, the "decapitation" strike, and "shock and awe" campaigns would become more or less expected and, thus, have become what we recognize as normal.

But wait a minute. In the previous examples, do we see Arthur wanting to have things both ways: being outraged when others break the rules but gaining glory when the rule-breaking is by his own hand? Maybe,

maybe not. In what may seem to be selective ethics, or even outright hypocrisy, Arthur's behavior can be understood—possibly predicted—given his moral grounding. His rule-breaking was based on his enemy's lack of ethics: the use of poorly trained and armed serfs as human shields. His quest for fairness (and victory) made the prospect of mowing down the front lines of peasants repellent.

When battle commanders look for opportunities to cut through the lines, they probe for zones that are poorly reinforced, the weak links. These chinks in the armor, so to speak, are viewed normally as the number and quality of troops and their equipment. Decisions about battle plans and the positioning of fighting assets are based on good intelligence-gathering; the plans and their implementation must be kept secret for as long as possible to maintain the element of surprise.

> *Merlyn had made suggestions about the way to win it, but, as these involved an ambush with secret aid from abroad, they had had to be kept dark. Lot's slowly approaching army was so much more numerous than the King's forces that it had been necessary to resort to stratagems. The way in which the battle was to be fought was a secret only known to four people.*[3]

This is why military commanders, business leaders, and legislators (and sometimes our relatives and neighbors) use disinformation and secrets to help gain a competitive advantage. In many circumstances, one can drive a wedge through a position better with talk than with tanks.

As Agravaine plotted with Mordred against Arthur, they quickly settled on a plan to exploit the king's blind spot, his personal chink in the armor. Arthur's unwillingness to acknowledge and address the affair between his wife and his best friend would provide the leverage his enemies needed to capsize his ship of state. Like so many before and after them, Mordred and Agravaine used scandal, or the threat of a concocted scandal, in an attempt to undermine authority and usurp control of the organization. They were going to catch Guinevere and Lancelot in the act.

> *"Arthur depends on Lancelot as his commander, and the chief of his troops. That is where his power comes from, because everybody knows that nobody can stand against brute force. But if we could make a little merry mischief between Arthur and Lancelot, because of the Queen, their power would be split."*
>
> *"Then would be the time to take your famous revenge."*[4]

The plot unfolded perfectly. Although he could have set aside the sentence, Arthur was compelled by his own ethics and his own laws to execute Guinevere. When Lancelot rescued the queen at the last moment (as Arthur had hoped), the two fled to France. Arthur, again, was forced to make a dreaded decision: he had to leave England and lay siege to Lancelot's castle. The trusting Arthur placed Mordred in charge.

The acting king was then free to move his plan to the next level. With control of the country's communications apparatus, he launched a propaganda campaign against Arthur in an effort to win the hearts and minds of the population.

> ". . . *Sir Mordred made write writs to all the barony of this land, and much people drew to him. For then was the common voice among them that with Arthur was none other life but war and strife, and with Sir Mordred was great joy and bliss. Thus was Sir Arthur depraved, and evil said of.*"[5]

Loyalty is never certain, never solid. Some people may harbor bad memories. Some people have a price. Some people are noncommittal and change their beliefs with the shifting political winds. Mordred capitalized on the "What have you done for me lately?" mentality to gain support and solidify his power base. Arthur, out of the country and unable to defend his good name, or remind the people of his vision and the progress made in achieving a more just society, was left to fight on two fronts. The wedge driven by Mordred cut deeply and left Arthur to resolve the personal issues with those he held most dear and to confront his son for the right to rule his own kingdom.

> *The situation became divorced from common sense, so that atrocity stories were accepted by the atrocious people. Many of the barons whom Lancelot had to put down had worked themselves into such a state about him, through fear of losing their ancient powers, that they believed him to be a sort of poison-gas man. They fought him with as much unscrupulousness and hatred as if he had been an anti-christ, and they truly believed themselves to be defending the right. It became a civil war of ideologies.*[6]

It wasn't just about Arthur, although Mordred and Agravaine certainly hated him. Lancelot was accused of being someone who "eats human children." It didn't matter that it wasn't true. Adversaries don't think twice about using unconventional tactics, fighting dirty, or spreading lies to distract or defeat you. The operating principle of Arthur's enemies was to take down anyone who was in their way. What made this all so effective was that enough people at court believed the lies. It was beyond reason, yet the alliance against Arthur began to solidify because of a belief system promoted by Mordred and Agravaine: the old way was better for them than the new. The betrayal could be justified because ideology ruled.

Authoritarians are most successful when they control the message and the communications infrastructure. Ethical leaders are successful when they invite coverage and expand communications. Dictatorial regimes don't attempt to control the media and the Internet for nothing.

Is there a way to combat the propaganda machine? It's difficult to defeat because once in place, misinformation is terribly difficult to retract and harder still to erase from one's memory. In a study of nearly 900 participants, researchers showed that "the repetition of tentative news stories, even if they are subsequently disconfirmed, can assist in the creation of false memories in a substantial proportion of people."[7] Once the information is published, "its subsequent correction does not alter people's beliefs unless they are suspicious about the motives underlying the events the news stories are about." And, "when people ignore corrections, they do so irrespective of how certain they are that the corrections occurred." The bottom line is that people may continue to rely on misinformation even when a subsequent retraction is made and remembered.

Surrounding your target audience with compelling information and compelling advocates—people who are trusted and known to be objective—can help to drown out or marginalize the propaganda. Then, there's fighting fire with fire.

King Mark, who was a mortal enemy of Arthur's knight Sir Tristram because of yet another love triangle (the famous story of Tristram and Isoud, or Tristan and Isolde), was a master of disinformation and circulated forged letters to make trouble for Arthur and his crew. Lancelot called him King Fox.

" . . . *for King Mark is so villainous, that by fair speech shall never man get of him.*"[8]

Sir Dinadan, a young knight eager to help his esteemed elders, devised a plan to undermine King Mark; he planned to give his adversary a taste of his own medicine. Like today's use of new media (blogs, Twitter, Facebook, and YouTube, for example), Dinadan used the best vehicle of the day to spread the word. He wrote a scathing and embarrassing song and unleashed it across Mark's lands. It was like a music video going viral across the Internet and then getting coverage by the mainstream media.

He knew that what was at one time popular or credible can become stale or implausible once something or someone becomes the butt of a joke.

Though punching, counterpunching, and trading attack ads using highly edited or out-of-context information are commonplace today, the Internet introduces a new level of threat to organizations and individuals. Incorrect or damaging information, sounds, and images can live forever in cyberspace unless there is a concerted effort to monitor and expunge the offending material. Filling such a niche are companies like Reputation Defender, that, for a monthly fee, will "defend your good name."

We have always needed to protect our information about finances, personnel, business deals, and new products or services. Now, cyberattacks, launched by enemies unseen from across the hall or across the globe, could disable a company or a country. On an individual level, there is cyberbullying. Public humiliation has never been made easier. At virtually no cost and with little planning required, seeking vengeance or retribution—"webtribution" as Elizabeth Bernstein wrote in *The Wall Street Journal*—allows us to give in to our impulses without thinking through consequences.[9] This is especially problematic for teenagers, who may not have the coping skills to deal with these kinds of assaults. Sadly, there have been suicides attributed to cyberbullying.[10]

The sheer volume of information that's being pumped into the ether is another kind of threat. It's increasingly difficult to differentiate the good data from the bad. In 2008, Google announced that its systems counted over 1 trillion unique URLs (uniform resource locators or domain names), up from 1 billion in 2000 and 26 million in 1998.[11] With each URL having at least one page and in many cases many more, the total number is just about beyond comprehension.

The problem of cutting through the clutter of information is exacerbated further by the public's uneven level of education. For example, in a National Science Foundation survey, only 10 percent of the respondents could properly define the word "molecule." Perhaps even more shocking is that nearly half did not know that it takes the Earth a year to orbit the sun and 20 percent believed the sun orbits the Earth.[12]

Without the ability to challenge the veracity of Web-based information, or any information delivered through any medium, people are left with taking things at face value. This is especially alarming when it comes to health and science, because the Internet has become a key source of medical information. Millions are making potentially life-and-death decisions on sometimes anonymous or bogus sources of information.

As our webmasters build a site for our organization, we need to ensure its credibility and do our part to gain the public's trust. The sponsor's name should be apparent, and directions for contacting someone in the organization should be straightforward. Depending on the type of content, information should be backed by one or more sources. Providing links to third parties is another way to demonstrate the organization's sincere intentions.

If you're an owner of information, it's obvious that you'll want to be on the first page of results of someone's Internet search. Yet the public may not always be aware that what comes up first on the list may not always be the best or most meaningful selection for them. Internet search engines use mathematical algorithms to determine the prominence of Web pages and factor in variables such the number and frequency of relevant search terms and the number of links to other pages and sites. What is supposed to be an impartial system, however, is gamed through search engine optimization (SEO) techniques. It's another bending of the rules, a more modern method of spreading unfiltered information.

While biased information and counterintelligence campaigns have an important place in diplomatic and military circles, it's a hard way to score points with customers or gain credibility with the public. When I was asked to develop a negative campaign targeted against a client's main competitor, I suggested a program to showcase the client's product instead. When they were fixed on impugning the other, however, I walked away. It's much less a question about someone finding out and exposing the plan, though that could be an embarrassing reputation-killer; it's about what is ethically correct and what is best for the business.

Communicating means reaching out to coworkers, subordinates, consumers, and constituents. It means asking, not waiting, and walking around, not sitting at your desk, and listening to the grapevine, not trivializing it. It's initiating as well as receiving; it's winning hearts and minds, not browbeating others into submission.

The need for communicating is ongoing—it never stops—and it's especially important when rumor, office politics, or deceit abound. When others "use cannon," it's up to you to track the source and determine whether or not a counterstrike is warranted. It's conceivable that a response could raise the issue to a more conspicuous level than if it were just left alone. If a response is appropriate, the next set of decisions should determine if it's visible and direct, or less detectable and indirect, potentially with the assistance of a third party. The possibility of legal action also needs to be weighed, but, again, the decision must consider the consequences of placing the proceedings in the public domain, extending the issue over an extended period of time, as well as the financial and human resource costs.

In a war on the battlefield or in the media, though, keeping the lines of communications open can keep hope alive for an end to the hostilities and a resolution to the conflict. An open door and genuine engagement are also the best ways to keep on top of the news that is internal and external to your organization. Essentially, it's the rationale to perform a never-ending audit: stakeholder research on moods, trends, and ideas.

As we covered in Chapter Six, best behavior and ethics are requirements for sustaining good business. Despite the potential for mixed messages in the examples in this chapter, it's not OK to change the rules when it suits you or your organization. It invalidates all of the trust you have built up over the course of your career. What is OK (and sometimes a necessity) is to adapt and change course (as we saw in Chapter Seven), and, when the conditions demand it, to use a few cannons of your own.

CAMELOT WISDOM:

- We may not want to acknowledge it, but it's an unfortunate reality that not everyone will share your ethics or sense of fair play. "Trust, but verify" is an operating principle.
- Once unleashed, it's devilishly difficult to retract or erase propaganda. Tracking the source and surrounding the offenders with compelling information, advocates can help to mitigate its effects.
- Responding to rumor or disinformation must be carefully gauged. Not responding and allowing the issue to cool may be better than striking back and fanning the flames.
- It's increasingly difficult to differentiate good information from bad. Arthur might have had more success against Mordred if his subjects had been better educated.
- Arthur found that loyalty can be fleeting. Despite our past accomplishments, we need to be cognizant of the "What have you done for me lately?" mentality.
- Insecure or autocratic leaders seek limitations on communications; responsible and ethical leaders seek to expand them.

CHAPTER 10

REALISM AND IDEALISM: BALANCING VISION AND EXECUTION

We've talked about teaching, grooming, and mentoring; being unwavering in maintaining fairness and high ethics; creating a strategic vision; confronting issues; and establishing open lines of communications. All of it is important, but none of it is always realistic.

We can never keep to the ideal at all times. We're flawed, just as heroes (real or imagined) find it impossible to always be up on the proverbial pedestal. John F. Kennedy and Dwight Eisenhower were adulterers, George Washington and Thomas Jefferson owned slaves, Winston Churchill and Babe Ruth drank to excess, and Indiana Jones and Captain Jack Sparrow loved their spoils as much as the adventures that always seemed to endanger others. The list goes on.

The conflict between vision and execution is sometimes difficult to balance. The days are gone when visionaries could charm Wall Street without any products or profits. The tech bubble burst in 2000 for good reason. At the other pole, it's difficult to be a leader—someone to inspire and motivate others—by sticking only to the details of execution. For this right-brain, left-brain approach—being in the trenches surrounded with details while dreaming about the future—we need to be thinking and operating in multiple dimensions, like being in an airplane with the ability to fly at different altitudes simultaneously. At one level, success is maximized when you're able to dive in and get your head and hands around the issue quickly. On another level, we must gain distance away from the nitty-gritty for unfettered thought and planning.

Our multiplanar airplane, of course, exists only in a perfect world. As much as we may wish, we can't be in more than one place at the same time and we can't go full tilt in more than one direction. (Churchill may have come close during the years of World War II, with his enormous grasp of political and military strategy as well as the minute details down to the number of chickens lost in a German bombing raid.) So, what constitutes the best-case scenario is, in reality, the endeavor to arrive at the most balanced scenario.

Where do we find balance in our approach to leadership and management? Is it an innate characteristic? Can it be taught or learned through observation? Is it derived from lessons learned as children? We are told that Arthur had been "beautifully brought up." But beauty, as the saying goes, is in the eye of the beholder.

> "*. . . he had grown up without any of the useful accomplishments for living—without malice, vanity, suspicion, cruelty, and the commoner forms of selfishness.*"[1]

In the environment of his youth, Arthur knew no balance. It's no surprise. Those responsible for our upbringing usually want to shield us from the cold, cruel world. For Arthur, learning about the ways of combat was more sport than preparation for adulthood. He thought his destiny was to be Kay's squire. But sooner or later, with or without the help of our parents, we're exposed to life's downs in addition to its ups.

There are big implications for "living in a bubble." Rising to the top of an organization—government, business, or academic—usually means being increasingly insulated from everyday issues and information (as we discussed in Chapter Two). They don't call it the top of the pyramid for nothing. There are even consequences related to health. Research has shown that living in a "too clean" environment, where a child is kept away from the normal, sometimes dirty environment, may actually increase the chance of developing certain diseases, such as asthma. This is known as the hygienic hypothesis.[2] If our immune systems aren't exposed to environmental antigens at an early age, we are less able to mount an effective response when confronted by them in the future. Indeed, our bodies may overreact to what might have been a fairly benign invader.

So we need that contact with the real world. We need to know the consequences of improper action or, just as meaningful, inaction. What's important is that all of the human dramas, including the unfairness and the cruelties, get put into a larger context of life experiences. We need all sorts of inputs from parents, friends, teachers, clergy, and mentors— even books, TV, radio, and the Internet—to help us along toward an understanding of right and wrong, good behavior and bad. Damage to our ability to gain perspective and balance can create the monsters of society: sociopaths who lie, cheat, steal, or worse.

Understanding that there is good and bad in people, whether it's in relationships or in business, allows us to be more aware and better prepared. And, as appropriate, it allows us to be more forgiving. Part of our experience growing older is learning how to take people as a whole. Remember, as discussed in Chapter Six, that we're a package. It allows us to mitigate disappointments but also to create positive, productive relationships. Anyone who has attended successive high school or college reunions can attest to this mellowing, this larger perspective. Some jerks will remain, and there will still be a bit of one-upsmanship, but, on the whole, people want to see the positives and reconnect. Teenagers and twenty something may have gotten Facebook off the ground, but it's the adults who seem to have taken over.

Thus, balance helps us as we find the common ground and create the important coalitions that broaden the base of support from which we lead. It's all about knowing how to take and amplify the good while recognizing and dealing with the bad.

We're social beings, and, to work most effectively, we must bring our social skills to the workplace. Being on our "best behavior" shouldn't mean that we're somehow faking it. Sugar-coating feedback so that the real intent is lost or pretending to show personal interest in a coworker's personal life isn't the answer. It's not as simple as "catching more flies with honey than you can with vinegar." We need to remain in character; we need to be our best selves.

> "... *all men of worship hate an envious man, and will shew him no favour, and he that is courteous, and kind, and gentle, hath favour in every place."*[3]

I believe that there are at least a few people "without a mean bone in their bodies," but most of us probably have a few spiteful skeletal pieces. Suppressing some of our more unkind instincts shouldn't take a lot of effort, however. Knowing right from wrong is to be expected. Yet, we are complicated beings, and many thoughts and emotions get caught up in the maelstrom of decision making. In an episode of the original *Star Trek* series ("The Enemy Within," 1966), a transporter malfunction splits Captain Kirk into good and evil twins. Neither can survive without the other; they must be recombined. The contrasting Kirks must be balanced in order to live and to function optimally. Being all good, not wanting to offend, is not the ideal condition when a commander needs to make quick, life-and-death decisions.

No, I'm not making excuses for cruel rulers. There is no "necessary evil." The point is that we need to acknowledge and confront our imperfections and cope with the imperfections of others. It's essential to good leadership.

If what is good can have varied definitions, then what about the issue of ethics? In Chapter Five, the point was made that adherence to ethics must be constant. But what is realistic? Do we need to cross the line occasionally to remind us of where the line is?

> *"Morals," said Lionel, "are a form of insanity. Give me a moral man who insists on doing the right thing all the time, and I will show you a tangle which an angel couldn't get out of."*[4]

The outburst by Lionel, one of Lancelot's cousins, was in reaction to his brother's behavior. When Bors found Lionel naked, tied up, and beaten with thorns by two knights, he chose instead to rescue a maiden. The maiden, Bors reasoned, was purer than his brother and, thus, more worthy of his aid.

Lionel correctly called this an issue of morals, one wrapped in Bors's religious beliefs, not ethics; the two can get confused. So, the ethical line still stands. It only moves when society moves it.

What is most clear from the Lionel-Bors conflict is that the two held different standards. (All was forgiven in the end. Lionel saw that Bors was undergoing a series of trials on his quest for the Holy Grail.) Holding yourself to one standard and your colleagues, staff, clients, or contractors to another could also cause conflict. The same goes with the way we treat spouses, children, and neighbors. Setting the standards, business or personal, and ensuring that all agree and understand them is a realistic expectation.

Mixed in with morals and ethics is truth. Here, again, truth is something that people, sometimes conveniently and selfishly, interpret all the time. Throw faith into this mix and you have a party. It's a discussion that's well beyond the scope of this book, but it's crucial that we recognize what is often a dynamic commingling of facts and beliefs.

> *When you are a scientist you must press on without remorse, following the only thing of importance, Truth.*[5]

Merlin didn't want Arthur to feel as though he had failed. His was but a first step, although Arthur didn't feel as though he moved the nation from square one. He wanted Arthur to recognize that his life and his life's work were a journey; it wasn't a straight shot from point A to point B. It's understandable that, with so many wrong turns and dead ends, we can lose sight of the progress that we made. Yet, we must keep trying; we need to pursue our truth.

Pressing forward and following through are essential leadership qualities. Although we've discussed the need to shift strategies and change tactics when circumstances demand, finishing the job demonstrates to staff, contributors, and investors that you have the ability to undertake the many phases of the business plan. From start to finish, you guided the organization with effective and timely execution.

". . . never let any other man complete a task unto which you yourself have set your hand."[6]

With the complexities of most business plans, and the compartmentalization of many organizations, it's common for subordinates to take control of certain pieces of the project. It's not realistic for executives to do everything on their own or to insert themselves into all aspects of the work.

This decentralization of authority requires delegation, and delegation requires the executive to empower others. If an executive has trouble delegating, it could be because there's insufficient trust of subordinates, a lack of talented subordinates, or an ego too large to believe that others can do the job adequately. If you're an "A" person, then you should have hired "A" people, people who are high performers like yourself. But, as my favorite HR saying (the ABC rule) continues, if you're a "B" person, it's likely that you've hired "C" people. If you want to get the job done, you'll involve others. If not, your ability to succeed will be limited by the number of people and projects you can oversee directly on your own.

Allowing the limelight to shine on others doesn't diminish you in the least. The members of your team will be able to share in the success of the organization. You'll acquire new loyalty and a stronger, more cohesive unit. The less competent and less confident will hog the glory by minimizing the contribution of others or even take undue credit. The theft of authorship or acknowledgment will be remembered (as I remember how some of the memos and reports I wrote on the way up the ladder were cut and pasted onto someone else's letterhead).

Employees rally around leaders who apply the rules fairly and communicate regularly and openly. People inside and outside the organization want to associate or collaborate with this kind of leader. And businesses want to do deals with this kind of leader. But, in addition to the alienation generated by the credit-grabbing leader, there's no quicker turnoff to employees than to be an inconsistent leader.

Sure, we need to be realistic about our ability to act in an ideal way all the time. Yet, it's so important to be consistent. Although we strive for and demand consistently good leadership behaviors, people seem grateful for just knowing what to expect from their bosses, even if it's a consistently rotten disposition.

The notion of balance that we've been discussing isn't some equation that averages out the sum of great decisions and poor choices. Arthur realized this when he recounted his attempt to kill Mordred when he was a baby; no matter what righteous acts he performed during the rest of his lifetime, Arthur couldn't mitigate the cascade of events brought on by his one evil action.

> *"Do you think you can stop the consequences of a bad action, by doing good ones afterwards? I don't. I have been trying to stopper it down with good actions, ever since, but it goes on in widening circles."*[7]

Arthur knew, too late, that "getting it right" the first time would have changed the course of history, including his own life, dramatically. No matter how difficult or complex a situation, or however challenged for time we might be, we can see the importance of adhering to the tenets of ready, aim, fire. That is, research and consider the options, define the plan and examine the potential consequences, and then execute the tactics. The plan, as we've discussed, needs a consistent hand but one that can also test the hypothesis, measure results, and change direction when needed.

Consistency can be viewed as plodding or unimaginative by some, but it can also be a ticket to power. (Of course, one can be consistently creative or fair or efficient.) Consistency means that the leader communicates the expectations for the business and the conduct of the staff. The boundaries and goals are clearly defined.

Consistency is not predictability, although repeating successful strategies, tactics, and behaviors can build a lasting legacy of achievement. Consistency is not longevity, although working and surviving in an organization long enough can bring the perks and power of seniority. The true power we derive from consistency, however, comes to us as ever-growing credibility, loyalty, and trust. With these key ingredients, we have the power to persuade and the power to lead.

We know that people respond to consistency in their leaders, but they also count on consistency when they choose friends, foods, and brands. Franchise operations bank on this fact. A particular franchise may not have the best-in-class service or product, but we know what to expect; we know that what we receive will be consistent no matter where or when we make the purchase.

Like other examples in this chapter, our ability to remain consistent needs a dose of reality. If we set too high an expectation, when the ideal is our only target, we're certain to disappoint ourselves and others the vast majority of the time. It's great to pay attention to the details. Perfectionism, to a point, is laudable. But there is such a thing as setting the bar too high. When we set the bar too high for others, we could be accused of setting people up to fail. When we set our personal goals too high and then fail to achieve them, we may end up with lower self-esteem. We may get depressed.

> *"Long ago, when I had my Merlyn to help, he tried to teach me to think. He knew he would have to leave in the end, so he forced me to think for myself. Don't ever let anybody teach you to think, Lance: it is the curse of the world."*[8]

Arthur was frustrated, worn out, and angry when he voiced his regret to Lancelot. Mordred and his brothers had just killed Arthur's friend King Pellinore (in retribution for accidentally killing the head of their clan, King Lot, in a tournament), and Mordred went on to kill Pellinore's son, Sir Lamorak, with a knife in the back. Might for Right was failing. Arthur was regretful that he started the messy journey. He wished that he could have left the thinking up to someone else.

We're often hardest on ourselves. We have to live with ourselves and face the mirror every morning. Still, if we live and love by setting high yet realistic standards, the regrets should be vanishingly few. Indeed, Arthur realized soon after his momentary breakdown that Might for Right was just a step. There was knowledge to be carried away from the experience that could be rethought and repackaged, and redeployed in a new and better strategy.

It's as simple as accepting Murphy's law: if something can go wrong, it will. It's simply not possible to plan for every scenario or always be able to predict all the outcomes of human behavior. We will make mistakes of our own accord, and mistakes will be thrust upon us.

An unpredictable situation erupted during the final battle between Mordred and Arthur, a battle waged after the malevolent and opportunistic usurper seized control of England in the king's absence. During a tenuous truce between the armies, it was understood that any hostile move would be interpreted as an act of war. So, when a knight got bitten by a snake and reflexively drew his sword, he inadvertently set off a bloodbath.

> *"And when the knight felt him stung, he looked down and saw the adder, and then he drew his sword to slay the adder, and thought of none other harm."*[9]

For most of us, our actions don't have the potential to spark a conflagration, but the important lessons here are to resist impulses and stay aware and understand the environment that you're operating in. The flip comment, the spontaneous gesture—they can now live forever on YouTube, a news channel, or an adversary's Web page.

It is difficult yet crucial to be able to balance thought and action. It pays to be vigilant with these two behaviors not only in times of war but also in our everyday lives—driving, working, or parenting. Not being so, drifting or lurching from one to the other, can be unwise and unhealthy, both mentally and physically.

A lack of both thought and action is another variation on this theme. It's the mindset we discussed in Chapter Eight: the abandonment of responsibility, the not wanting to deal with a situation, or not wanting to know when things go awry. How many of us have wished a situation would just go away? When faced with a messy conflict or a potentially lose-lose situation, looking down into a hole in the sand can seem attractive.

"I didn't want to be conscious of it. I hoped that if only I was not quite conscious of everything, it would come straight in the end."[10]

Arthur expressed his regret to Gawaine that he hadn't been more direct with Lancelot and Guinevere. Mordred was able to learn of the affair and use the scandalous knowledge as a weapon to undermine the king. It gave Arthur no good options: his wife would have to face death as an adulterer, his friend and commander of his armed forces would be gone, and Equal Justice would fail to flourish because of all the preoccupations.

"What was Right, what was Wrong? What distinguished Doing from Not Doing? If I were to have my time again, the old King thought, I would bury myself in a monastery, for fear of a Doing which might lead to woe."[11]

As we've discussed, Arthur was a courageous and kind leader but could not come face-to-face with the emotional trauma of confronting the affair between his comrade and his wife. He made many hard choices during his reign, but he became deaf and blind to what ended up mattering the most. It wasn't a war that defeated his ambition, a vision not for himself but for England. It was a failure to overcome his ultimate discomfort. It was not his own embarrassment that he worried about; it was the thought of embarrassing others. Maybe an airing of the situation would have driven him mad. We know that Lancelot snapped when he learned that he was duped into sleeping with Elaine (when he thought he was bedding down with Guinevere). We won't know what might have happened with Arthur.

Experience shows us that, while a face-off isn't pleasing, there is usually more pain involved in not doing than in doing. It's the anticipation of what might happen that gives us the most anxiety. Things percolate. Problems churn. They can heat up and cool off and then heat up again. Ultimately, they boil over, and we can't get the scalding water back into the pot. You have a crisis on the stovetop.

Ideally, issues never become problems. They should be identified and dealt with prior to their development into real dilemmas or emergencies. When faced with a serious issue or a longer-term crisis, the parties involved communicate openly and move quickly toward a resolution. Realistically, though, people will often choose comfort and expediency. Hoping, wishing, or praying for a particular outcome won't hurt, but they're not a substitute for addressing an underlying problem.

To operate efficiently and fairly, we need to prepare ourselves for confronting the problems, and the people who caused them, by coming to grips with uncomfortable situations promptly. How we choose to deal with issues and crises will either exacerbate or minimize the ultimate outcome. The time to respond and the tone of the communication matter more than the severity of the issue. People will remember that you were responsive and available for comment. They'll remember that executives, the decision makers in the organization, were involved personally and held themselves accountable. They'll remember how your words made them feel, not the words themselves. The goal is to get it right quickly, not eventually, even if you had no direct involvement during the genesis of the mess. And it doesn't mean getting even if you think you were wronged.

Such was Arthur's approach. He was generous in his forgiveness and pardoned many a transgression. In his attempt to adhere to his ideal, Arthur let Mordred off the hook instead of meting out harsh punishment. We know that he couldn't allow himself to punish Mordred again. He tried once when Mordred was a baby, and the sin followed him for the rest of his life.

Realistically, though, we may feel the need for some payback or a reward for having endured the assault. We yearn for justice. Still, reading how Mordred slithers through Arthur's grasp makes us want to yell, "Don't do it! Can't you see he's evil and needs to be stopped?!" Forgiving an enemy can have positive, peaceful ramifications, of course. There may be a strategic, legal, or political reason for raising the flag of truce. Whatever the motivation, it can sound a new tone, it can reset a relationship, and it can save lives, careers, and money. Although we need to remember history, we also need to move on. Carrying a grudge can create undue stresses on individuals as well as the business, with potentially negative effects on the work and health of both.

Striking the right balance when confronting people and issues means that one shouldn't dwell or dither, nor should one obfuscate or humiliate. A good, effective leader has the courage to move forward with a timely solution forged with reason and the input of others.

CAMELOT WISDOM:

- Leaders need a left-brain, right-brain approach to balance vision and execution. The most balanced scenario is best.
- Acknowledging and confronting our own imperfections, coping with the imperfections of others, and providing clear feedback can create better relationships and more productive partnerships.
- Progress does not always occur in a straight line. Merlin helped Arthur realize that his life and his life's work were a journey. With all the twists and turns, it's easy to lose sight of the progress we have made.
- Setting standards and maintaining a consistent approach are crucial. Holding yourself to one standard and the rest to another is duplicitous.
- Arthur had little trouble delegating, but many leaders find it difficult to either trust or find enough talented subordinates to manage effectively. Otherwise, the ability to succeed is limited by the number of projects you can oversee directly.
- Few of us go looking for a confrontation, but there is usually much more pain and consequence in not doing than doing, as Arthur's life demonstrated. The anticipation and anxiety of what might be are the usual barriers to facing the problem. Getting it right, not getting even, is the best way to resolve conflicts.

CHAPTER 11

JOUST FOR FUN: DEALING WITH BOUNDARY ISSUES

Arthur was a determined king. With serious purpose, he took great risks in an effort to ensure that his subjects were treated fairly. He developed grand plans, fought wars, and cajoled nobles along the twisted, thorny path toward Equal Justice. He also realized that all work and no play would make Arthur a dull king.

Where work and play intersect, and how involved executives should be in the lives of their subordinates, are important considerations. How familiar is too familiar? When does office camaraderie erode authority? Some organizations are clear about where the lines are drawn. Others are much more causal: it would be impossible to pick out the executive from the mail sorter in a lineup.

Arthur was known to take the occasional break and hit the reset button with the people at court. With all the tension swirling around him—the internecine strife as well as the threats from beyond his borders—Arthur would occasionally leave the worries of his office behind for an activity that allowed him and his knights to blow off some medieval steam. Jousting tournaments, pitting man against man, or hunts, pitting man against beast, were the preferred team-building experiences. Our modern commanders-in-chief also require some pleasant diversion, but usually with a lot less blood.

> *"You will have to have special Feasts," interrupted Kay, "at Pentecost and so on, when all the knights come to dinner and say what they have done. It will make them want to fight in this new way of yours, if they are going to recite about it afterwards. And Merlyn could write their names in their places by magic, and their coat armour could be engraved over their sieges. It would be grand!"*[1]

Having celebratory events and creating opportunities for internal recognition are great ways to show your appreciation and raise the spirits of the organization. Arthur was quick to bestow high praise and acknowledge the achievements of any deserving person. Too often, though, we overlook employees as a key audience or stakeholder. In business, where success is often founded on forming positive relationships, we are terrible at saying thank you. Win or lose, a thank you to staff (not to mention vendors, consultants, or anyone else who had a stake in the effort) is both the cheapest and richest expression one can offer.

I was reminded of this after I wrote a blog article about the passing of Martin Delaney, the founder of Project Inform, a San Francisco–based HIV/AIDS treatment and public policy advocacy organization.[2] Someone commented that he liked the sentiment very much but asked if I had ever told Marty just how meaningful our interactions were to me.

Marty and I met not too long after Project Inform was founded. I was directing HIV/AIDS public policy and communications at a global pharmaceutical company, and he was on the other side of the table. With antiretroviral drugs in the pipeline, seeing the emerging influence of AIDS activist groups (and the break-ins and boycotts affecting a competitor company), and imagining the potential benefits of hearing the patients' point of view, I pressed the company for engagement. I remember quoting Lincoln to my management: "As our case is new, so we must think anew, and act anew."

There was no playbook. Pharmaceutical companies didn't interact with consumers back in the 1980s. The company would inform the "learned intermediary," the physician, and he or she would communicate with the patient. Marty helped to dispose of that dogma and enhanced the dialogue between all of the key stakeholders. The industry and the FDA grappled for years over ways to expedite the review and approval of drugs for serious or life-threatening diseases. Marty helped to change policy, and many thousands of patients were able to gain early access and benefit from new therapies.

Working with Marty helped me to learn a key lesson, one discussed earlier in Chapter Seven: the importance of finding the common ground. The world was changing. The normal course of business, the normal course of life, was disrupted. We, the industry, and the patient community approached our goals from different directions using different strategies and tactics. But much of what we all sought was the same. Our constituency was their constituency, and everyone wanted new medications on the market as soon as possible. The two "sides," jointly, worked to expand drug access and education programs, increase the enrollment of patients into clinical trials, and reauthorize research incentives like R&D tax credits and the Orphan Drug Act.

It wasn't always pretty or easy. There were wrong turns and bumps in the road, but at least we were on the road together, held there by mutual interest and mutual respect. Yes, Marty knew that I appreciated him and his work, but somehow I feel that I could have been more concrete. We should never wait to show our appreciation.

Sharing the good news (and bad) and acknowledging others shouldn't be delayed within the corporate community, either. It's an important element of any internal communications function. If a corporate culture values connectedness, and a free exchange of ideas and information is desired, then inward-facing communications must be a priority for management.

As we share the news and the glory, we must also think about sharing the spoils. Although many attach a high value to just receiving the recognition—the "psychic glory"—there's an expectation of a more tangible reward for outstanding performance. Lunch with the boss, a corporate gift (sometimes from a catalog), or a plaque may have their places, but they frequently underwhelm. It's no surprise that time off from work is one of the most welcomed rewards.

Leaders and high performers tend to work long hours at stressful jobs. Time to rest and satisfy other interests—family, hobby, and travel—enables both brain and body to recharge. Even so, there are many who fear that their job might disappear or be given to another in their absence. This might be a real possibility if the company is struggling, or it might be imagined because of a lack of confidence. The "I can't take vacation because (1) the place will fall apart without me or (2) I need to be seen and not forgotten" syndrome afflicts executives and staff alike. The hours and days of accumulated vacation pile up and sometimes expire; time and enjoyment that cannot be recaptured.

For the knights, their work was their life. Life is more compartmentalized today, although some people don't ever want to go home; they don't want to face what waits for them and, thus, use work as a refuge. Clearly, the workplace should not be the only source of social interaction or emotional support. Professional counseling might be appropriate; otherwise, I have told staff, "If you don't have a life, go and try to find one." Taking the allotted vacation time is a criterion on the performance reviews I conduct.

Still, it's money that is the most welcomed. Money may not always buy love, but it can usually buy a fair amount of happiness and security. Arthur and his allies, however, were more predisposed to a type of wealth redistribution.

When it was delivered to Ban and Bors, they gave the goods as freely to their knights as it was given to them.[3]

After the battle with the 11 Kings, Arthur's allies made a fair and equitable distribution of the king's reward to his knights for their part in the victory. There was no "me first" or free-for-all grab of the booty. It was a deliberate process. A similar occurrence was common with kidnappings and ransoms. Abductions were prevalent in the Arthurian literature, and, when Arthur's knights overthrew the wicked captors, their treasure would be split among the captives.

In many sectors of our economy today, lavish pay and bonuses are sometimes disconnected from performance. Golden parachutes, corporate jets, and country club memberships have incited choruses of discontent as workers, investors, and politicians demand that top corporate executives shed some of their trappings and realign their compensation with the value they deliver.

Arthur Levitt Jr., former chairman of the U.S. Securities and Exchange Commission, declared in an op-ed in *The Wall Street Journal* in 2005 that "The Imperial CEO Is No More."[4] Too many executives have thought themselves indispensable and, thus, worth their king-sized pay packages of seven or eight (sometimes even nine) figures a year. He wrote that "this decade's investors are looking for something more nuanced, a balance" that is best characterized by "lower-keyed but hugely effective leaders." Rather than the take-no-prisoners, everyone-else-be-damned approach, society needs CEOs who are "thoughtful and sensitive to the public obligations of the private sector," "corporate leaders who don't think of themselves as the soul of their company, but who do their part to help create a company with a soul."

(Perceptive words, though Levitt is an adviser to Goldman Sachs, which pays its CEO like, well, a king. Indeed, financial journalist Gary Weiss wrote in his blog that "Goldman and the rest of the Street owe Levitt, big time. When he was chairman of the SEC, the agency did absolutely nothing to regulate derivatives or hedge funds, did nothing to rein in executive compensation, took only tepid steps to curb brokerage sales practices."[5])

> *They saw no man at all, but England.*
> *"A king is the head of his people, and he must stand as an example to them, and do as they wish."*[6]

The CEO embodies the organization. Investors, financial analysts, and donors look carefully at top management when making their decisions to buy, sell, or donate. Their performance and their reputation, as financial stewards and stewards of the corporate culture, have become part of the equation of business valuation. Setting the example by using power wisely and doing what's best for all (or for the majority), not the individual, has become more acceptable and more favored than greed.

Arthur was attuned to the needs of others because of his famous empathy. He was, after all, one of the people. He was just a country kid when he was suddenly catapulted onto the throne. Arthur was more than comfortable with the working class. He showed respect and friendship to the kennel keepers, the stable staff, and the kitchen cooks.

There is a risk in being too close, however. Aside from the more talked-about issues of office romances or sexual harassment, there are more subtle interactions that can have a negative effect on the organization and the effectiveness of its people. There are risks to "letting your hair down" with the staff and pretending to be just one of the guys or gals. It's similar to parents who want to dress and act like their children. A parent might be acting out of jealousy or attempting to recapture his or her youth, but the similarity lies in a confusion of roles: the need to be liked, to be their friend rather than their parent.

All sorts of conflicting messages can be sent in an honest attempt to connect with staff. Employees may start to ask: Why is the boss hanging around us so much? Is there an expectation that we should be asking the boss out with us? How can we be ourselves with the boss around all the time? Does this mean we can get some special treatment? How seriously do we take this person who is trying too hard to be liked? It pays to tread carefully.

It's one thing to interact and relax at a company kegger, but it's another when the interactions are too forced. You can't mandate fun or good morale. I was in a room full of executives at a leadership retreat when the moderator asked, "What is your job?" The answers from the group were varied and included: "I protect and expand the reputation of my company," "I generate new business and keep the money flowing in," and "I try to create a great atmosphere where the people can contribute, learn, grow, and have fun."

Wait, what? Fun? How much fun should we be expected to provide? Directly, none. Someone's fun or happiness is his or her own job, or the job of a friend or spouse. Fun, like morale and office friendships, should be the happy byproduct of a vibrant, empowered work environment.

Lancelot was Arthur's best friend as well as a key employee, given his status as military commander and the chief protector of the king and queen. It was a difficult position for both him and the king. They didn't have the raw discussions or exchanges of ideas they needed because one wanted to spare the feelings of the other. The truth was choked back, and, thus, they were undone in the end. It's crucial that the work environment allows for the delivery of advice and opinion that may run counter to the CEO's beliefs. Diverse opinions or the hard truth must be made available to ensure that the available options are considered.

Everyone has a role to play in the organization, yet not all players may have an equal understanding of their roles. Problems can arise when the roles aren't explicit or when players are uncomfortable in their position. Arthur knew his role well, but his responsibilities weighed on him mightily. He was England, and if the country was to move forward, together as people toward Equal Justice, he had to do the pulling. Unfortunately, there were no other advocates as passionate as he and no other force that could match his power to effect change. We should not have to face such a lonely challenge today.

It's to be expected, then, that Arthur had the periodic yearning for simpler times. He escaped by hosting the occasional tournament and would shed the fine furs and fashions of royalty to dress in common clothes. Generally, he was quite casual in his speech and in his daily interactions as well. It can be refreshing to see powerful, influential people, while maintaining appropriate boundaries, not take themselves too seriously. This didn't sit well with Merlin, however. He insisted that Arthur assume the right role of king, including the airs and pomp.

> *"Go away!" he shouted. "What are you doing here? What do you mean by it? Aren't you the King of England? Go away and send for me!"[7]*

Merlin wasn't advocating that Arthur adopt a harsher demeanor. He didn't want Arthur to make the mistake we see too often today of attempting to use fear and intimidation as a way to gain respect. Executives who behave that way believe the deference they observe is respect, but it is not. They're viewed as what they are: bullies. Their accomplishments might be impressive, but as people they are not.

Merlin didn't want the king leaving his office to call on him; it was more appropriate for him to go to the king because appearances and perceptions are important. Of course, "managing by walking around" and stopping in the office of a subordinate is more or less expected today. Still, there are different responsibilities and accountabilities, and, like it or not, there are boundaries in the workplace that must be respected. Arthur knew this. Despite the image of a boundary less Round Table, there was "the head of the Table," and Arthur sat at it.

Whether it's a conscious decision or one made out of ignorance, people cross the boundary lines, both ways, all the time. The consequences vary depending on the infraction, but too many times there are few to none.

A breakdown in barriers and behavior (and good sense) can occur because people and organizations aren't willing to set limits. There are too few that will object when that line, wherever it is in society or within a particular institution, has been crossed.

People can blame the "fringe" for bad behavior or chalk it up to the narcissists who believe that boundaries should bend around them. And some will blame it on emotion, but we've all heard the tired and wholly inadequate excuses: "I'm a very passionate person," "It was just a sponta-neous outburst," "My emotions took over." Fine. But did anyone speak out? Once, maybe twice, might be forgiven, but anything else is a pattern that needs to be interrupted.

Perhaps a particular boundary-breaking incident occurred at an event that was not sanctioned. "We can't be held responsible for the actions of individuals" goes the refrain. Historically, there have always been unsanc-tioned events that occasionally damaged the reputation of the employer, but now there are nearly an infinite number of ways for boundaries to be crossed—at a political rally, support or a advocacy group, you name it.

It's conceivable that Merlin, the seer and sorcerer, may have prophesied the Internet, but we know that he never told Arthur about it. The ways to discuss, review, praise, and criticize each other and our institutions are too numerous to count. What might be viewed as "just for fun" or a way to air some feelings could have unintended consequences. We have never known a more powerful tool to generate and perpetuate gossip.

Arthur was very measured in his communication; his outbursts were few. He may not have always been comfortable in his role, but he respected the office. As king, setting the example for Equal Justice, he always thought the best of people; he felt that intentions were almost always honorable. Although rumormongering is not exactly an honorable pursuit, there are things to be learned from listening. Unfortunately, Arthur ignored this important source of information.

Political correctness, sexual harassment lawsuits, and the Internet have made the issue of boundaries much more complicated than in Arthur's day. Of course, we can have workplace friendships that extend into our personal lives, but they're usually more appropriate for peers. Those in charge should not be "friending" their staff on Facebook, unless they have a desire to be called "creepy" or labeled as a "stalker."

Societal, institutional, and personal standards must keep us aware of the many invisible but genuine lines of conduct, because behavior still counts. Unless you want to be known as a beast, you are harming your personal brand, or the brand of your organization, by engaging in uncouth (or potentially unlawful) behavior. We all know that part of successful reputation management is setting the proper tone for communication. Manners can trump message.

Like it or not, leaders are role models; they set an example. Without any impediments, bad behaviors are bound to be emulated and propagated. And bad behavior can incite worse. With each unchecked incident, the line separating good behavior from bad gets shifted and a new, potentially dangerous norm is set. In the most extreme case, it seems that the threshold from outburst to threat or from threat to violence is getting unsettlingly easy to breach.

CAMELOT WISDOM:

- Arthur was quick to praise the achievements of others. Internal recognition and a thank you to others who contributed to organizational efforts are important expressions of gratitude that leaders must remember to offer.
- Although jousts and hunts may not be appropriate, it's important for all hard workers to rest and satisfy other interests so that both brain and body can recharge.
- As a corollary, it's laudable that some devote so much of their lives to their work, but the workplace should not be the only source of social interaction or emotional support.
- Showing compassion and empathy for staff is important, but it does have its limits. We must be wary of sending conflicting messages as we try to form connections with others.
- Though Arthur's Table was round, he sat at its head. Even in so-called flat organizations, there are boundaries and appearances that need to be maintained.
- Fun and good morale cannot be mandated; they are outcomes of an honest, communicative, and interesting work environment.
- Having the boss as your friend may inhibit the delivery of divergent opinions or hard truths. As Arthur and Lancelot knew, sparing some feelings to preserve a friendship can end up wrecking both the friendship and the organization.

CHAPTER 12

DUTIFUL VERSUS INSPIRED THINKING: BEING INSIDE AND OUTSIDE THE BOX

The Round Table, as we've discussed, was a brain trust, a communications vehicle, a police force, and a symbol for chivalry and brotherhood. The Quest for the Holy Grail was designed to channel the energy of the Knights of the Round Table and unite them in a common mission. Attempting to turn the concept of Equal Justice into a new civil code was an effort to change the very nature of civilization and the relationship between the government and the governed. These actions were all inspired, visionary concepts of King Arthur, a man who had been raised to be a squire, the attendant to his knighted stepbrother, Kay.

This greatness—Arthur's creativity and vision—were not foregone conclusions, however. Merlin spent years helping him to learn life's lessons and to appreciate the perspective of others (sometimes in a surreptitious manner and sometimes at the peril of the young Arthur). The combination of a good heart and a good head allowed Arthur to eventually synthesize all of the inputs—the issues, the rules, the personalities, and the history of his time—and reformulate the soup of information into a concoction of his own making: a new vision for England. But it was not an easy road.

> *"I suppose you will learn some day," he said, "but God knows it is heart-breaking, uphill work."*[1]

Discovering new ways to approach old problems—this is what Merlin was discussing with Arthur. It was going to be a difficult journey to convince the people of the age to adopt a new mindset and transition away from war as a method to settle all scores. Sometimes we need to learn "the hard way" and experience failure and misery before finding the best solution. Sometimes we find a spark that ignites a whole series of creative fires, and sometimes the ideas come after a long process of grinding through piles of data. Whatever the pathway, the learning process is never over.

"It is not so much what you are doing," he said. "It is how you are thinking. If there's one thing I can't stand, it is stupidity."

"If I have done something stupid, tell me. Don't be in a bad temper."

"Tell you!" he exclaimed. "And what is going to happen when there is nobody to tell you? Are you never going to think for yourself?"[2]

After years of tutelage, Merlin had to force the issue of self-reliance upon Arthur. It's hard to tell if the mentor was running out of patience or out of time. (Perhaps they should have discussed expectations at the beginning of their relationship.) Whatever the reason for Merlin's agitation, the bottom line remained: someday Arthur had to rely on his own devices and critical-thinking skills to lead the nation.

We don't spend enough time thinking about thinking. We hear the terms along the thinking spectrum—concrete, narrow, analytical, strategic, and creative—but rarely consider which type might be most important to leadership or the type of thinking that is most indicative of success. And, to make matters more complicated, there's also critical, ideological, logical, ordered, and group thinking. With all these available labels, what kind of thinker was Arthur?

The old man had always been a dutiful thinker, never an inspired one.[3]

What was meant by this? Was this an insult? Is there an implication that dutiful thinking is inferior to creative thinking? Whatever the intent, I'll take exception to this assessment of Arthur's thinking.

A dutiful thinker is a habitual thinker, one who is always observing, searching for solutions, and attempting to anticipate the future. Arthur fit this description. He never stopped trying to satisfy Merlin's mandate to be thinking all the time. Dutiful thinking, steady and stepwise, is a virtue of its own.

Peter Drucker, the iconic management and leadership expert, wrote in the concluding chapter of his breakthrough book, *The Effective Executive,* "What is being developed here, in other words, is leadership—not the leadership of brilliance and genius, to be sure, but the much more modest yet more enduring leadership of dedication, determination, and serious purpose."[4] It's interesting to note, too, that habitual thinking isn't just a good leadership practice. It's a form of mental exercise that, over a lifetime of consistent contemplation, changes our neurological patterns.[5, 6] More time thinking helps to remodel our brains so that we get better at thinking.

One who perseveres and chips away at a problem until it's reduced to a manageable nugget deserves great credit. Carl von Clausewitz, the 19th-century Prussian general and father of modern military strategy, wrote in his epic *On War* that "if we were to ask what sort of intellect is most closely associated with military genius, observation and experience inform us that it is the analytical rather than the creative mind, the more all-encompassing than the narrowly focused mind, the cooler rather than the hot-tempered mind that we should more readily entrust in war with the well-being of our brothers and children, and the honor and safety of our country."[7]

Usually, the best ideas come from the insights derived from solid information, those bits of data that can be gleaned from factual sources and research. Although there are many ways to obtain information (such as published works, interviews, surveys, observation, and experimentation), T. H. White broke idea generation down into just two categories: the dutiful (which we can call synthesizers) and the inspired (which are the outside-the-boxers, or OTBs). Both approaches, of course, can be successful. Or not. And both can be found within the same individual, but to varying degrees.

Albert Einstein was a full-bore synthesizer *and* an OTB. His thinking, of course, was nothing short of breakthrough; he was truly a genius for all time. After placing his famous theories on the table, however, Einstein sought a way to bring them together into a Unified Field Theory, or "the theory of everything," a way to understand all the forces of nature with a single, elegant explanation. It was called Einstein's Holy Grail.

> . . . *there were three kinds of law to be wrestled with. He was trying to boil them down, from Customary, Canon and Roman law, into a single code which he hoped to call the Civil one.*[8]

Like Arthur, however, Einstein never found what he was looking for. His plan failed. Arthur's attempt at a unified theory—to combine and reform the laws of his day—was also taking something that was accepted and crafting something new and better. They both provided the spark; we know it wasn't all for nothing. Others would come and build on their achievements.

Distilling ideas, plans, or numbers into workable models is an important pursuit and a valuable form of creativity. Think of the time saved or the new opportunities uncovered when the clutter of information we face each day can be filtered and recategorized into more usable forms.

A perverse form of creativity takes the opposite approach: making things as complicated as possible so that it's devilishly difficult to penetrate and comprehend a scheme's inner workings. This might be motivated by an effort to (1) make oneself indispensable by being among the exceedingly few who can decode the matter of mystery or (2) circumvent an existing law or regulation. Such shenanigans, like credit default swaps and other complex financial derivatives, had a hand in causing the Great Recession of the late 2000s. Using genius and innovation to clarify information rather than cloud it allows our work to become more available and palatable for consumption. It's keeping things as simple as is appropriate, not dumbing things down. We need to make things more transparent, more accessible, and more obvious.

> *"What are your most important members?"*
> *"My wings."*
> *"The answer ought to be feet. . . ."*
> *"Because these beasts depend upon the powers of their feet, so that, by law, any damage to the feet of a hawk, hound or horse, is reckoned as damage to its life."*[9]

To the peregrine running this particular Q&A session lesson, the answer was clear. For Arthur, having been newly transformed into a bird (a merlin, actually), the quick answer was also obvious: obvious to a boy, obvious to someone with concrete thinking, and yet wrong. Ideas can be good or great, but they need to match the time, the place, and the environment. What's the most important part of a bird? Clearly, birds need their wings to fly. Yet a hawk is a "beast of the foot," requiring its feet to catch and strangle its prey. Ideas, and answers, are situational.

It's true that the obvious is usually that way for a reason, and the intuitive response, the gut reaction, is often a very good guide to the correct solution or behavior. We've all been there. We know that in some situations there's little time to think, only time to act instinctively. Indeed, many times it's good to have some very simple rules to guide us.

> *There was only one rule in boar hunting. It was: Hold on.*[10]

When face-to-face with a powerful, wild animal with sharp tusks pointed in your direction, you have few options. Stay or go. In this case, thinking "inside the box" can be the difference between life and death. And, like so many other situations, the follow-through is critical. If you should separate from your hunting party, you can become the prey. In a business or organization, if you give up, if you falter, you may find your role reversed from acquirer to target. If parts of a coalition fall away, so may the big opportunity, and a mighty effort can crumble. If you fail to persevere, your competitors might outlast you.

So, what's the difference between thinking like a synthesizer or an OTB? The synthesizer is a terrific aggregator of information who compiles, analyzes, and reorganizes data into a workable platform. That reformulation of information and ideas may be novel enough to create a new product, relaunch a mature brand, or make the difference in winning a deal. Synthesizers are resourceful and sometimes underestimate their creativity. They can poke holes in existing plans, find new sources of information, and repackage old ideas into fresh ones.

Being an OTB doesn't mean that anyone has to fit a particular stereotype for what "creative" looks like. There are plenty of flamboyant-looking out-of-the-box thinkers, but the exterior package matters little. Women don't have to wear mounds of big jewelry, nor do men have to sport a ponytail. I know top public relations and advertising agency people who look like they came out of a Brooks Brothers or Talbots catalog, and a few real-life spies who are anything but James Bond.

Aim high when you shoot in battle, rather than low. A low arrow strikes the ground, a high one may kill in the second rank. [11]

Where did this bit of battle wisdom come from? Arthur didn't hear it from Merlin or Lancelot or any other member of the Round Table. It was given by Marian, often referred to as Maid or Lady in the literature, of Robin Wood's band. Great thinkers and great leaders eschew stereotypes because they themselves don't fit any particular mold.

Classically, OTBs ask, "What if? Why are things the way they are? Can we look at this from an entirely different point of view? What else do we need to know?" OTBs are less satisfied with the *status quo*, the current foundation of information, and rely more on open-ended questions to spur thought, discussion, and new tangents.

Arthur learned the value, even the freedom, that questions can bring, especially when the utterance of a query was viewed as a treasonous act. Independent thought was not an option for the ants he visited during one of his early lessons.

EVERYTHING NOT FORBIDDEN IS COMPULSORY

. . . there were only two qualifications in the language, Done and Not-Done—which applied to all questions of value.

A question was a sign of insanity to them. Their life was not questionable: it was dictated.[12]

The ants have been a successful life form for many millions of years with their binary language. Arthur, of course, had a hard time with this concept. He was utterly surprised and repulsed by their lack of individuality and independent thought. Decisions in the human world are rarely as easy as "must do, must not do." We require more nuance, more options, to navigate through our professional and personal lives.

". . . the only thing worth doing for the race is to increase its stock of ideas. Then, if you make available a larger stock, the people are at liberty to help themselves from out of it. By this process the means of improvement is offered, to be accepted or rejected freely."[13]

Some people, though, are just fine with being told what to do. Or, they're satisfied with the information they already have. Indeed, going beyond a certain amount of information could prove to be too much. Instead of seeing new options, the additional data could paralyze their thought process. Although some leaders have been known to fall into this category, good leaders aren't part of this picture. Without probing questions, there will be no new ideas. We'd be left only with monotony and repetition. We'd be more like the ant drones that Arthur encountered than strategic thinkers and doers.

Asking questions includes asking for the input of others. Some creative thinkers, especially in public relations and advertising agencies, have been elevated into positions such as chief creative officer. You may have also seen the titles creative guru, creative ninja, or even head of creation (which may get an argument from, shall we say, a higher authority). I have known a few who took their titles to mean that creativity was their personal domain and theirs alone. These individuals would go into seclusion so they could develop "the big idea." Then, they presented their concepts as a *fait accompli*, like Athena bursting out of Zeus's head fully armored and ready for battle. The need to protect one's positions and validate their continued employment is understandable. You want and need exceptional thinkers on your team, but they have to realize that there is, or should be, a team. Without good leadership from the "creative types," the other human resources in the organization will be wasted and demoralized.

On the other hand, some executives want to concentrate the thinking and idea generation in their organizations. People have their strengths and weaknesses, after all, and everyone should have a defined role. Besides, if things go wrong, axing the "idea man" can be a convenient way to show action and to deflect blame and responsibility.

Just as creativity exists along a spectrum, the process of creativity also has variations on a theme. Some people and organizations may be predisposed to self-reliance and individual efforts, whereas others may favor teamwork and multidisciplinary groups. Again, they are not mutually exclusive. The best leaders know how to balance both approaches. One way to blend these two seemingly disparate styles is to channel the process of idea generation.

Yes, there is a process to being creative. Touched on in Chapter Three, a leader facilitates and guides the brainstorm: people who can contribute to the effort are chosen, regardless of their level or grade; roles and responsibilities are assigned; agreement is reached on the goals and objectives; the key stakeholder groups are defined; available budget and resources are specified; and background information is prepared and distributed. Then, after the ground rules for the brainstorming session have been discussed, it's time for the actual ideas for strategies and tactics to begin to fly in an organized process.

So, how important is original thought to good leadership? Well, it's really important. We have to bring something new to the table, don't we? It's one of the things that helps separate a great leader from a great manager. A survey released in 2010 by IBM of more than 1,500 CEOs from 60 countries and 33 industries emphasized that even "more than rigor, management discipline, integrity, or even vision—successfully navigating an increasing complex world will require creativity." Creativity was cited by 60 percent of the CEOs as the most important attribute; integrity was next at 52 percent.[14] With such a high premium placed on creativity, the CEOs in the survey signaled some concern because less than half of them "believe their enterprises are adequately prepared to handle a highly volatile, increasingly complex business environment."

This may not be a staffing problem. It could mean that there are just not enough creative thinkers to go around. Indeed, there is some evidence to suggest that we may be heading for a creativity crisis. A review of nearly 300,000 creativity tests, also called Torrance scores, of children and adults collected over several decades showed that American creativity has been declining since 1990.[15] (These tests were based on the work of the late E. Paul Torrance, an educational psychologist best known for his research on creativity.) However, as we've noted, creativity is in the eye of the beholder. There's more than one definition and more than one way that creativity can lead to success. Still, we must ensure that our educational system emphasizes idea generation and problem-solving techniques in addition to the more traditional memorization and drills.

It brings us back again to the issue of balance. We need to operate and think back and forth on a continuum. There is a time and place for the detailed plan as well as the half-baked, and a time and place for thinking about conventional tactics as well as the flashy and unconventional. Individually, we all tend to skew in one direction or the other. Even so, an analytical thinker can have a creative flash, and the creative thinker may have some concrete thoughts.

End-to-end creativity may not always play a role in an organization's success, however. A creative deal or program may be essential to win the new business deal or endear you to management for your out-of-the-box concept, but the "nuts and bolts," the tried-and-true tactics, seem to get funded the majority of the time. Most people, whether they're in management or shopping in the mall, will gravitate to the safer, more familiar, and less risky choice. A track record, a history of costs, and the validation of others are powerful persuaders. They carry proof, not just potential. It's often the old stand-bys that can act as cash cows to help fund the riskier, more innovative projects. Pharmaceutical companies, for example, spend billions marketing products (with billions more flowing back in revenue) with little or no incremental benefit over other medicines to help drive their costly R&D efforts forward.

The grand visions and promises of the dot.com boom eventually gave way to the more traditional focus on products and profits. The pull between form and substance needed to find a healthier equilibrium, balancing creativity with execution. Unfortunately, what's been referred to as a "burst bubble" in 2000 felt more like a volcanic eruption. There were too few people asking questions, just as there were later in the decade. The Great Recession was caused, in part, by the lack of questions, follow-through, and oversight. Thus, there's no coasting allowed in leadership, no resting on laurels, and no blaming others for organizational blunders. Leadership isn't about leaving the controls on autopilot. The same old, same old is not acceptable.

After General Motors and then Toyota reached the top of the automobile business, complacency set in. GM fell behind the innovation curve over the course of many years. Toyota's reputation, on the other hand, seemed to skid off the road suddenly when a failure to acknowledge problems with brakes and unintended acceleration ballooned into massive recalls in 2010. Leaders and their organizations can't let their guard down, and they can't stop observing the conditions inside and outside their walls.

Is there a better way to think? Was Merlin right about Arthur? Yes and no. Like most things in life, there's a time and place for different types of thinking. You are not deficient or inadequate if you are not recognized as the most "creative" force in the room. We are who we are. We just need to understand that contributions can be made across the thinking spectrum.

The conflict between synthesizers and OTBs is artificial, fed by egos that yearn for the acknowledgement and reverence of others. Despite our highly competitive ways, we need a fusion of ideas, not a contest with a winner and a loser. Once people begin to believe that they've cornered the market on innovative thinking and intelligence, it's time to call a time-out. Remember Enron from Chapter Eight? The so-called "smartest guys in the room" oversaw the collapse of the seventh largest company in the United States in 2001. And, as mentioned previously, the fraud and corruption scandal also brought down the Big Five accounting firm Arthur Andersen.

Being highly intelligent does not mean that you're a good thinker, a good leader, or a good anything else. It takes a yearning to learn to be a good thinker. We need information from our colleagues, from those above us and below us in the organization, and information from anywhere else that could impact the potential success or failure of the enterprise. In business, being creative takes work, discipline, and perseverance.

"So my Table was not a failure—Master?"
"Certainly not. It was an experiment. Experiments lead to new ones."[16]

Arthur, undermined by his son and at the brink of his final battle, was depressed at the unraveling of his life's work to unify his country. Merlin provided some comfort by reassuring his student that all the hard labor was worthwhile; it will carry forward. It was a step in an evolutionary process.

Nevertheless, it must have been a terrible blow to Arthur. Instead of reaching the summit of peace, he found a valley of despair. It can be disheartening to any of us to see our vision trampled or discarded without due consideration. It's hard to accept, but it's a rare event to give birth to a complete solution on the first try. Very few ideas are fully formed and functioning in the way they were first conceived. Reaching the final product is usually a (sometimes exasperating and painful) process of compromise and negotiation. Sometimes it's a better product for all of the inputs. Sometimes all of the tinkering causes it to be unrecognizable from where it all began.

It's hard, but try not to weep over your ideas that go nowhere or for those that do end up somewhere but mutated and spoiled without you. The button will not always be yours to push. It may never be. Executives in the service industries, for example, must leave it up to their clients to make the final decision. There are too many wonderful, powerful ideas to count that lie unused. They may gather dust for eternity, get resuscitated at another time, or possibly be repackaged for some other, potentially related use.

As we saw with Lancelot's perseverance to become the best knight and with Merlin's constant picking at problems, we need to think about our challenges and opportunities on a daily basis. Leadership calls for dutiful thinking, thinking that is habitual, clear, and organized. Thinking that can cut through some of the gray and find unclouded sky. Thinking that enables the creative process to flourish.

CAMELOT WISDOM:

- The learning process is never over, whether it's learning the "hard way," soliciting ideas from others (above and below), or grinding through piles of data.
- Arthur had a steady and stepwise approach to problem solving. Habitual, dutiful thinking—always observing, searching for solutions, and attempting to anticipate the future—is a critical leadership activity.
- We must use our skills to clarify rather than complicate things so that issues and ideas are more transparent, more accessible, and more obvious.
- There is a process to creativity. Information about the challenge, audience, objectives, budget, and resources must be provided before the strategies and tactics begin to fly.
- As much as we may pride ourselves on our abilities to generate great ideas, few are born fully functional. Reaching the final product or solution may be a painful but necessary process of compromise and negotiation.

CHAPTER 13

PASSING THE CANDLE: PLANNING FOR SUCCESSION

Everyone wants to enjoy personal success, but leaders have the added desire and responsibility to ensure the ongoing success of their institutions and, even more broadly, their constituents or communities. One way to help guarantee the organization's financial sustainability and cultural durability is to engage in careful succession planning for the top executive as well as other key officers and managers.

Few doubt the importance of good process and orderly transition. A 2010 survey by the National Association of Corporate Directors asked board members which three governance issues were the most important. Of the 20 options available, the top five included executive talent management and leadership development, and CEO succession.[1] A separate poll showed that nearly half of the companies with revenues greater than $500 million have "no meaningful" succession plan.[2]

The reasons are varied, but they could be viewed as a microcosm of human psychology, ranging from feelings of fear about being bested by a replacement to the delusion of one's invulnerability and the indispensability of one's skills. Some sitting CEOs don't want to deflect attention from themselves, nor do they want employees to go prematurely to the heir apparent for decisions that might undermine their current authority.

No one (except perhaps in the case of the parent-child relationship) is indispensable. Founders pass on, executives are recruited elsewhere, military officers are wounded in battle, sports stars get injuries, and yet, life and the organization move on.

No one can know why Arthur failed to plan for his own succession. After the showdown with his only son, Mordred, he was left with no direct heirs. (Like many other aspects of Arthur's life, this has been contested. Some stories recall one or more, most likely, illegitimate children.) And, well before the battle, he had some clear signs of his son's treachery. In his later years, it's possible that he was incapable of looking forward because of his depression. We can't give him a clinical diagnosis, but he did despair that his goals for England went unfulfilled. Of course, he accomplished much more than he realized during his reign, but there were so few who could appreciate his ideas and contributions. He came close so many times to achieving his vision, if only—if only he had closed those leadership loops that we've discussed throughout this book.

Perhaps Equal Justice would have spread wider and faster if Arthur had planned for his succession. Instead, the king was left to his last desperate option. He called upon his young page, 12-year-old Thomas (White's tip of the hat to Sir Thomas Malory, author of *Le Morte d'Arthur*), to keep the ideas burning after his life flickered out.

> *"You see, the King wanted there to be somebody left, who would remember their famous idea."*
>
> *"Will you try to remember that you are a kind of vessel to carry on the idea, when things go wrong, and that the whole hope depends on you alive?"*
>
> *"Thomas, my idea of those knights was a sort of candle, like these ones here. I've carried it for many years with a hand to shield it from the wind. It has flickered often. I'm giving you the candle now—you won't let it out?"*
>
> *"It will burn."*[3]

What a mighty crapshoot for Arthur to rely on a young boy in the last moments of his life to preserve such a momentous political and societal vision! Not to mention that this passing of the candle took place in the middle of a war zone; the boy could have been killed, and then it would have been game over for Equal Justice for who knows how long. A slightly different end, however, is depicted in *Le Morte d'Arthur*.

> *"Ah my lord Arthur, what shall become of me, now ye go from me and leave me here alone among mine enemies? Comfort thyself, said the king, and do as well as thou mayest, for in me is no trust to trust in."*[4]

Arthur, mortally wounded, told the only person available, in this case Sir Bedivere, to do the best he could and not to look upon him for any further guidance or insight. Again, succession planning was nowhere in sight. In the account of Arthur's last moments written by Howard Pyle, however, we see some semblance of postmortem instructions, although we are not privy to what they were. This time it's up to the king's squire, Boisenard, to carry the message forward.

*"And if I do not return in a month from this time . . . thou mayest tell Sir
Constantine of Cornwall that he is to search the papers in my cabinet, and
that there he will find all that is to be done should death overtake me."*[5]

No one counseled Arthur on the matter of who and what should have
come next, despite his reputation for encouraging and accepting input
from his court. For whatever reason, there was collective denial of the
obvious and inevitable. Even the military, an institution known for its
succession planning, failed to act appropriately. Adding to Arthur's
horrendous oversight, there was no plan to replace Camelot's top commander, Lancelot.

*"Thus they endured in great penance six year; and then Sir Launcelot took
the habit of priesthood of the Bishop, and a twelvemonth he sang mass."*[6]

After Arthur was gone, Lancelot went into a long period of mourning and
repentance. He didn't step up to the plate to help stabilize the country or
fulfill Arthur's ideals. He, too, was too damaged by the psychological burden
of betrayals and what-ifs that complicated his life, threatened his dearest
friends, and unhinged his soul. It's a pity, too, that so little was learned
from the passing of the previous king, Arthur's father Uther. Arthur, and
the rest of England, had a very poor role model in this regard.

*And after Uther-Pendragon had departed from this life, it was likewise as
Merlin had feared, for all the realm fell into great disorder. For each lesser
king contended against his fellow for overlordship.*[7]

The infighting and power-grabbing that Arthur abhorred was doomed
to repeat—a pattern that seems to occur in family-run organizations
perhaps more frequently than in other ownership categories. Many don't
have the size or depth of leadership to effect an orderly transition, and
there could be issues of sibling rivalry, favoritism, divorce, and/or contested
wills.

Large corporations, too, can be threatened by family succession issues.
When DuPont president Henry du Pont died in 1889, the company was
left without a leader; the family patriarch had failed to designate a
successor, and there were no obvious candidates for the job. As time wore
on, DuPont was nearly sold to a competitor before three du Pont cousins
engineered a buy-out in 1902 to keep the business in the family.

In contrast, Stew Leonard, the dairy-store tycoon (mentioned briefly in
Chapter Six), did have a succession plan. His surprise was that it had to be

implemented so quickly. Although he was groomed for the dairy business by his father, a fatal heart attack put Leonard and his brother suddenly in charge of a nine-person operation. He came to understand, however, that learning the business and having a plan for the business were two different things.

Leonard, with a showman's guile, took the family dairy and built it into a small chain of mega-stores. With his four children involved in various aspects of the business, he took steps to install his eldest, Stew Jr., as company president. The title became more than ceremonial when the Internal Revenue Service began investigating a 10-year, $17 million tax fraud scheme. Stew Jr. brought together all of the employees for a storewide meeting and cemented his new position of leadership. (The senior Leonard was sentenced to 52 months at a minimum-security prison camp.) According to Stew Sr., "He reassured everyone that the company was strong and that their jobs were secure. Stew [Jr.] demonstrated that he was the strong and secure leader I knew he was. His leadership inspired the respect that everyone, especially his siblings, had for him."[8]

Though not for long. Younger brother Tom, who was running one of the Disney-esque supermarkets, felt underappreciated and became resentful. Eventually, he faced tax fraud issues of his own and separated from the company. Sometimes the best plans are upended by human unpredictability.

Toyota transitioned to nonfamily executive leadership from 1950 to 1967 and again from 1995 to 2009. The last shift back into family hands was a publicly aired saga of buyer's remorse. After quality problems hit the car company hard (as mentioned in Chapter Twelve), the Toyoda family, led by the grandson of the founder, blamed the regime of outsiders. Akio Toyoda complained that some of the company's leaders "just got too big-headed and focused too excessively on profit."[9] Toyoda, however, didn't seem to oppose the profit and growth strategy when the company surpassed General Motors as the world's largest auto manufacturer. The former chief of Toyota's U.S. operations, Jim Press, defended the family and said, "The root cause of their problems is that the company was hijacked, some years ago, by anti-family, financially oriented pirates."[10]

Illness or death, legal or regulatory issues, the stated need to spend more time with family, expired terms, greener pastures, or a change of heart can all upset succession plans, if there were any to begin with. In the case of Hewlett-Packard CEO Mark Hurd, it was falsifying a series of expense reports that involved a relationship with marketing contractor and former actress Jodie Fisher. While there was no evidence of sexual misconduct, the board moved swiftly to remove Hurd in August 2010 in what it said was a demonstration of equal application of its ethical code across all levels of the company.

Larry Ellison, CEO of Oracle, called the ouster "unexplainable" and a "loss of one of Silicon Valley's best and most respected leaders." Ellison hired Hurd as a company president about a month later, triggering a lawsuit from HP that alleged a violation of Hurd's severance agreement to protect confidential information. On the other side, Jeffrey Sonnenfeld, senior associate dean at the Yale School of Management, said HP "made a courageous call. There may not be a legal issue, but there is still a moral issue," he added.[11]

The financial impact was immediate. HP stock fell more than 8 percent on the news, wiping out $8.7 billion in market value. Hurd, however, received a severance package worth an estimated $35 million but later waived about half the amount in a settlement of the lawsuit. The upheaval also left the firm with no clear successor. The uncertainty lingered as the board formed a CEO search committee and then held a competition between executive search firms to determine which one would aid their selection process. A new hire came less than two months later, however, when HP tapped former SAP CEO Leo Apotheker in favor of internal candidates.

Some executives have no choice about when they move on, and others know when it's time. Going out on that "high note" helps to preserve one's ego and legacy, whether it's in business, entertainment, or politics. Problems can erupt, though, when you know it's time but others may not be as informed. Bank of America's board of directors had to convene an "emergency succession committee" when CEO Ken Lewis announced his resignation in 2009.

Not so with A. G. Lafley. He was riding high as Procter & Gamble's CEO when he transitioned into a new role as executive chairman in 2009. When Lafley was elevated into the CEO spot, he set a new tone that was notable for going against type; the former Navy officer leaned toward the Arthurian style, with a more casual manner, and was not the usual CEO-king found in so many corner offices. So, when P&G veteran Bob McDonald was named the new CEO, Lafley gave him the attention and space he deserved and required by moving out of the executive suite and into an office nine floors below. After the board voted to confirm McDonald, Lafley and the new CEO called customers and investors and held "town hall" meetings with employees across the globe. It all went according to a plan designed by a succession team with assistance from the board.

The intensive and deliberate succession process was the opposite of Lafley's own ascension, which came without warning following the ouster of his predecessor, Durk Jager. Lafley said his "transition was arguably the poorest in the history of this company."[12]

P&G, with a reputation for pushing talent up the ranks, took additional steps to ensure that its talent pool was well stocked and well fed. Referring to P&G's "Talent Portfolio," a binder with names and analyses of the company's future leaders, Moheet Nagrath, head of global human resources at P&G, said, "Today I could show you the next generation of successors to current leaders, the generation after that, and the generation after that."[13]

When the public "horse races" for leadership positions become protracted, rivalries and hard feelings are bound to emerge. In the three-way race to succeed GlaxoSmithKline CEO J. P. Garnier, the contenders were given various special assignments and were evaluated by an outside group of consultants, in addition to the board of directors. After naming Andrew Witty the winner, GSK tried to keep Chris Viehbacher and David Stout on board by naming them to the board. Stout chose retirement instead. Viehbacher agreed to stay but soon reversed course and became CEO of rival pharmaceutical powerhouse Sanofi-Aventis.

With nondisparagement agreements and an aversion to burning bridges under an umbrella of political correctness, few executives sound off against their institutions. Spite is not looked upon favorably by current or potential new employers.

"And we must keep the feud living forever."[14]

Though Arthur did his best to co-opt the negative elements in his court, he could not overcome the deep divisions with his own family. This ended up being his biggest barrier to any succession planning. Nephew Agravaine sought to prolong the feud; he couldn't forgive Arthur for his father's sin (of violating his grandmother, Igraine) from decades past. It didn't matter to him just how far the Pendragon acorn had fallen from the tree. Uther was a rapist, a representative of yesterday's time. Arthur was empathetic; he was the emblem of the future. Arthur broke the cycle, unlike Agravaine's mother, Morgause, who passed down some of her malevolence. Preserving and bettering the institution should be the primary concern and the common goal.

There are always winners and losers, but, with public succession contests, the visibility and scrutiny of the competition are magnified. When the media report that top management is being "shaken up" or that roles are being "realigned," it may be code for big changes ahead. The scramble begins, favorites are picked, and odds of success are deliberated. The world knows that some of the named contenders will be passed over. With a sense that their ability to operate effectively has been damaged, the also-rans often fold their tents and move to a different camp.

Although the subsequent brain drain may not be welcomed, the weeding-out process might have been a well-planned and desired outcome. This tactic could allow the new CEO the uncontested authority he or she may need to implement change in the organization; the potential people impediments are eliminated. In the well-known case of CEO succession at General Electric, Jack Welch and the GE board chose Jeffrey Immelt to be his successor in 2000, leaving Robert Nardelli and James McNerney as runners-up. With GE's deep pool of talent and strong leadership-development programs—practically a CEO incubator—Welch said that any of the top three contenders could have run the company. "We had three Gold Medal winners, and only one Gold Medal to give," he said.[15] Nardelli became CEO of Home Depot and then Chrysler, and McNerney became CEO of 3M and then Boeing.

When Mordred couldn't become the new ruler, he didn't think about moving to a rival kingdom with the idea of offering his services or taking over; that was a nonstarter. It wasn't about having his own plan for leadership; he just wanted what was Arthur's. Simply put, what should have been a series of steps toward a new vision for England was instead a bloody mess. The whole situation was so distracting that only dumb luck was able to rescue the king's grand vision at the last moment. Planning would have worked a whole lot better than procrastination.

Ready or not, the need for succession planning and execution is going to come. Although we can find many of Arthur's outstanding qualities and initiatives to emulate, his highly consequential inaction to prepare the next generation of leaders is not one of them.

CAMELOT WISDOM:

- Succession for executives and managers must not be left to chance; evaluation of internal and external talent, along with a predetermined, orderly process for transition, is required to help guarantee the organization's ongoing success.
- Barriers to succession, such as delusions of invulnerability or indispensability, need to be recognized and addressed.
- Public "horse races" for corporate/institutional leadership can help make the process transparent but may also create unwanted rivalries and ill will.
- Indecision and/or a failure to confront issues can confound the succession process just as any other.
- Personal issues need to be left at the castle. Arthur's vision for England was nearly lost because of family feuds and distractions.

CHAPTER 14

DESTINY AND LEGACY: MAKING YOUR PERSONAL AND PROFESSIONAL MARK

We want our work to count for something, however we want to define what that something is. It might be societal, like Arthur, who wanted a better existence for his people. It might be spiritual, like Lancelot, who wanted to serve God and render miracles. Or, it might be materialistic (with a dose of antisocial personality disorder), like Mordred, who wanted to best his father and accumulate power. For many, the effort, sacrifice, and hours of devoted work away from home, family, and friends (if you still have any) need to be offset by something meaningful and long-lasting. We have a deep-seated need to ensure that our value outlasts us. Being remembered helps us (perhaps fools us) into thinking that we have a chance at immortality.

In our younger years, we may not care about our legacy as much. There's plenty of time to address it later. Or maybe we never thought about starting out on the leadership path. We might not have had big thoughts or dreams. Surviving, getting by, earning enough to pay the rent, buying a car, or getting married might have been all that mattered or what we could have seen from that early vantage point. But things change. We might encounter an inspirational boss or mentor. An article, a blog, or a book might plant a new idea in our heads. Attractive new career choices evolve and become available, and opportunities might just fall into our laps; we were lucky enough to be in the right place at the right time.

The opportunity, though, may not be welcomed initially. When his foster brother Kay was about to be knighted, Arthur began to make peace with his upcoming role. He even boasted that he'd be a better squire than Kay would have been. Still, Arthur would have dearly loved to be included in the secret ceremony that Kay was about to experience.

"Only fools want to be great."[1]

Why did Arthur want to become a knight? What was the attraction? Was it just the expectation of the time? The message Merlin conveyed to Arthur was that it's important to understand why you feel how you feel. Greatness, or a title or an honor, in itself is not the real prize. Arthur, though, was still a teen, and he had a simple case of boyish envy. Merlin, knowing what was to come, was attempting to get his charge to put his life, all lives, into perspective.

What came next for Arthur was his destiny. What Arthur wanted was to be a knight. He wasn't looking for power, unlike Kay, who lied about pulling the sword from the stone. Indeed, after Arthur pulled (and replaced and pulled) the sword from the stone to prove that it was he that did the deed, he was full of woe, not wonder.

". . . I would rather have my father than be a King!"[2]

Arthur considered Ector to be his father. He knew nothing of Uther and didn't want to give up the only family he knew. It spoke to Arthur's character and where he placed his values. Destiny was not a welcomed caller; he probably would have preferred to have determined his own future. If Ector had lived a few centuries later, he could have quoted Shakespeare to his suddenly distinguished son: "Be not afraid of greatness: some are born great, some achieve greatness, and some have greatness thrust upon 'em."[3]

It was now up to Arthur to play the hand he was dealt to the best degree possible. He was pulled into the family business with the twin disadvantages of knowing nothing about the family or the business. Having the keys to the kingdom handed to you, literally, may be a dream for some, but not for this new king. After the surprise and the initial rejection by some of the nobles, Arthur gained his footing, accepted the new and weighty responsibilities, and began his reign.

It didn't take long, with the help of his mentor, for Arthur to lay the groundwork for a new and better approach to governing and to the treatment of the citizenry. If all went well, he knew that his legacy was to be the outcome of his mission, vision, and values (as discussed in Chapter Three). There were plenty of distractions (and disasters) along the way, but he never lost sight of the goal. He wasn't aiming for a legacy, but for an outcome. A legacy, similar to the issue of morale or happiness in the workplace from Chapter Eleven, is the lasting outcome of the effort and work attached to one's professional and/or personal life.

"The bravest people are the ones who don't mind looking like cowards."[4]

Too often, people are preoccupied with their image of the moment; they're afraid of "looking bad," or they're obsessed with the latest poll results. They shift with the political winds, or go with what's immediately gratifying or expedient, a short-term, shallow approach of conducting a long-term campaign—business, political, or otherwise. People have been told to "be yourself" or "stay true to yourself" for good reason. When Lancelot was locked in his castle after rescuing Guinevere, he was mocked by Arthur's army for not coming out and fighting like a man. Lancelot wouldn't take the bait. He was willing to look like a coward to avoid a direct confrontation with his still-cherished Arthur and to help keep the bloodshed to a minimum.

Arthur knew, through Merlin, that he had a destiny to fulfill, but he lacked some crucial details. He wasn't given all the answers, and he wasn't privy to the ending. It's a good thing, too. How would he have changed, what actions might have been altered or abandoned, if he knew what awaited him at the end of his journey?

> *Looking back at his life, it seemed to him that he had been struggling all the time to dam a flood, which, whenever he had checked it, had broken through at a new place, setting him his work to do again.*[5]

If he had only looked at the conclusion, he would have missed all of the other areas where he had a powerfully positive effect on people and their way of life. Believing that the future is completely out of your control is a great way to justify an abdication of responsibility or a ready excuse to behave badly.

Arthur expected the best from people. He thought adversaries would accept his logic and, if not fall in with him, at least move to a neutral, nonthreatening position. We know it was not to be. But instead of relishing the successes that occurred here and there, he felt like a failure; no matter how hard he tried, there was something to block his progress: one dead end, and one conflict, one disappointment after another. Although it's endearing that he cared so much about others and took his work so seriously, his compassion and naiveté conspired to create disappointment. He would have been a happier, more fulfilled person if he had thought a bit more about all the vested interests that his plans affected and planned for and around their agendas. Unfortunately, nobody took Arthur by his ermine-trimmed shoulders and said, "Scite happens."

This is why a skilled and talented team, third-party advocates, and a succession plan are necessary to carry a plan and a legacy forward. The success of the deals you engineer, the quality of the products you make or the work you produce, and the fairness and ethics of the people you hire all reflect on you.

How you lead your life also reflects on you and your organization. It may even be a predictor of performance. The conspicuous consumption of some executives led to a recent analysis that compared the values of the principal residences of all S&P 500 CEOs with their companies' stock performance.[6] The authors found that "future company performance deteriorated when CEOs acquire extremely large or costly mansions and estates," "a result consistent with large mansions and estates being proxies for CEO entrenchment." It's also interesting to note that when these CEOs held on to their company shares, their stock performance was significantly better than the stocks of firms whose CEOs liquidated their equity to finance their new homes.

Most CEOs work very hard and earn their way to the top. It was a horse race to the finish line, and then it's a horse race to acquire the nicest toys. Wanting the good life, a proper reward, should be expected. In the context of one's legacy, though, the excesses of wealth might help to distinguish them in a negative manner.

> *For it needs not that a man shall wear armor for to be a true knight, but only that he shall do his best endeavor with all patience and humility as it hath been ordained for him to do.*[7]

The trappings are great if there's taste and proportion involved. They shouldn't be begrudged (much). This matters little, however, to what is truly consequential to a legacy. The question isn't "How much did they make?" but "Did they exceed all expectation of delivering results?" "Were they fair, principled, and ethical?" and "Did they think beyond the boundaries of their organizations and care about their community?"

There are times, however, that you need to take advantage of your position and do what needs to be done to keep things moving forward. Leaders are not ordinary, nor are their means to affect change. In charge of a business, an institution, or an electorate, leaders are held to a higher order of responsibility.

> *". . . thou art not as an ordinary errant knight, but that thou art a King, and that thy life belongeth not unto thee, but unto thy people."*[8]

Arthur, always attempting to be fair and just, wanted a more level playing field for his people. This mindset included the field of battle.

He was disgusted to learn that Excalibur gave him special powers—it could slice through virtually anything (according to some accounts)—and wanted to throw the sword away to fight his battles on an equal footing with his adversaries. Merlin, though, was strongly opposed to such a rash act and won the argument. Arthur must be safeguarded because it was not only his life that was at stake. If he possessed an enchanted sword to help him stay on his righteous course, then so be it.

Leaders may not possess powers as exceptional as Excalibur, but they need to know how to apply them wisely and judiciously, nevertheless. Overkill can be vulgar and wasteful. A velvet hammer might be more appropriate than an iron fist.

> *Excalibur shone with so terrible a brightness that the very sight thereof would shake the spirits of every wrong-doer with such great fear that he would, in a manner, suffer the pangs of death ere ever the edge of the blade had touched his flesh.*[9]

Threats can be as sharp as Excalibur's blade and cut just as deeply. A sharp tongue and sharp elbows can, in some instances, get you out of a sticky situation and give you a reputation as a savvy entreprenuer. Or they may characterize you as obnoxious and intimidating. Flexing to the situation, and judging the necessity and the intensity of your weaponry, will require some Camelot wisdom. Success may come, but the costs—to the bottom line, to your staff, and to your reputation and legacy—need to be calcuated carefully. Just don't declare victory too soon.

> *"For I would not have you declare yourself to the world until you have proved your worthiness by your deeds. Wherefore, do not yourself proclaim your name, but wait until the world proclaimeth it; for it is better for the world to proclaim the worthiness of a man than that the man should proclaim his own worthiness."*[10]

The Lady of the Lake, a magical person who, in some accounts, presented Arthur with Excalibur, gave some good advice to Lancelot. (In this story, the Lady of the Lake also gives Lancelot a ring that could nullify any enchantment.) Lancelot had just received his knighthood and was ready to begin his new role. After reaching the peak of a new achievement, it's natural to feel pumped and proud and to toot one's own horn a bit. Praise out of one's own mouth, though, leans toward conceit. Allowing others to judge and laud your deeds elevates its credibility and demonstrates your humility. Without a modicum of modesty, we can quickly begin to believe our own PR and trust in our own infallibility.

Was it the wicked leaders who led innocent populations to slaughter, or was it wicked populations who chose leaders after their own hearts?[11]

If one is pumped up by ego, reality can become skewed; admitting mistakes is wrongly viewed as a sign of weakness. So, when plans do go off the tracks and your legacy is at risk, what can be done? Who can you blame? Such a person may never ask, "How am I responsible, what must I do to correct the situation?" Instead, the only explanation is that it must be someone else's fault. "If only they did or didn't do this or that, I wouldn't be in this mess" might go the self-absorbed logic. Turning a situation back on others—your competitors, your staff, or your family—is manipulative and revisionist. Arthur would not have approved of this unkind and unfair behavior.

Legacies are put in jeopardy all the time. Arthur knew at his end that a lifetime of achievement and honorable living can't always mitigate even one (momentous) wrong. Sandy Weill pieced together what was at one time the world's largest bank. The promised synergies of Citigroup, however, failed to materialize, with a consequential impact on the creation of this century's Great Recession. Despite his departure from the company in 2006, Weill is forever tied to the collapse of its stock price from $55.12 in May 2007 to $1.03 in March 2009. Hoping to defend his legacy, Weill sought a return but was rebuffed by the board of directors.

Deprived of using the Citigroup story to seal his reputation, Weill has tried to push the spotlight onto his philanthropic activities, having donated about $800 million over the years. It's an enormous sum, and it will likely buy at least some of the goodwill he is looking for.

Microsoft founder Bill Gates has had a better time of it following his departure from day-to-day operations. Although Microsoft had been recognized for good leadership and financial results in the past, public approval of Gates's philanthropy helped to propel the company to the number one position in Harris Interactive's Reputation Quotient in 2006 (up six positions from the previous year).[12] This isn't a final verdict on Gates's legacy because the survey looks year-to-year at the ups and downs of dozens of firms. (As a case in point, the 2009 survey saw Microsoft drop back to number seven, with Berkshire Hathaway assuming the number one position.[13]) But it's a lesson that you can't just throw money at a situation to improve a particular circumstance. It's who you are as a leader and person, and how you apply your resources.

Sometimes who you are, though, can be purposefully altered for posterity. A legacy can be engineered, or rescued, at least to a degree if an organization can be mobilized to do it on your behalf. George Steinbrenner, the former shipping tycoon, turned his $10 million investment in the New York Yankees baseball team in 1973 into approximately $1.5 billion at the time of his death in 2010. A 150-fold increase in value, seven World Series wins, and a new $2.3 billion (including $1.2 billion in taxpayer funding) state-of-the-art stadium (built in 2009 to replace the 1923 structure), are about as good as it gets in sports or any business. A great and memorable legacy assured, right?

Amazingly, probably yes. Amazing when one considers his brutish, despotic demeanor, that he gave illegal campaign contributions to Richard Nixon, that despite the new stadium he helped to build he also tore down a monument to baseball, "The House That Ruth Built," and fired beloved Hall of Fame catcher Yogi Berra, who was the team's manager, after just 16 games into the 1985 season. Steinbrenner apologized 14 years later.

In 1990, Steinbrenner was banned from baseball by Major League Baseball commissioner Fay Vincent after he paid a gambler named Howie Spira $40,000 to dig up "dirt" on Dave Winfield, a Hall of Fame outfielder who had sued the Yankees for failing to pay the Winfield Foundation $300,000, a figure guaranteed in his contract. (Many credited General Manager Gene Michael with building the championship roster during Steinbrenner's absence.) Steinbrenner was reinstated in 1993, but Spira remained bitter. "He ruined my life, my health and my reputation," he told *The New York Daily News*.[14]

Steinbrenner relished being called "The Boss," though the moniker was first applied by *Daily News* columnist Mike Lupica, a longtime antagonist. And it was to honor this mafia don-like devotion to his franchise and its success that New York City mayor Michael Bloomberg announced that all flags would be lowered at City Hall at the time of his death. This is the crux of the legacy rescue mission. It wasn't about his worthy philanthropic assistance to children of police officers and firefighters killed in the line of duty. It was about protecting baseball's reputation and the future value of the Yankee franchise, as well as its thousands of direct and indirect employees. With the official baseball seal of approval, capped by a seven foot high, five foot wide plaque that dwarfs everything else in the new stadium's Monument Park, Steinbrenner's legacy has been cemented. Major League Baseball commissioner Bud Selig said, "He was and always will be as much of a New York Yankee as Babe Ruth, Lou Gehrig, Joe DiMaggio, Mickey Mantle, Yogi Berra, Whitey Ford, and all of the other Yankee legends."

"Because a man can push you off a horse with a stick, it doesn't mean he is a better man than you are."[15]

Being brawny, a bully, or a billionaire does not determine one's worth. Nor should it bear on one's self-worth. Mordred rationalized his inferiority to Lancelot, but, in doing so, he provided a small pearl of wisdom (and unknowingly agreed with Merlin, who had grumbled earlier about the value of athletics versus scholarship). It's not about the lance or the horse or the armor. The assessment needs to be about who's holding the lance, who's riding the horse, and who's wearing the armor.

Although Arthur came up well short of seeing the full benefits of his great ideas and deeds, it shouldn't discourage us from pursuing our dreams and attempting to right any wrongs from our past. We can and should acknowledge the past while charting the future.

We cannot build the future by avenging the past.[16]

When efforts to rectify the past overwhelm or cloud our ability to move forward, we need a jolt to place us back on the right track. We can't sacrifice future efforts by dwelling too long on what may be a fool's journey to undo history. The war in Iraq might be in such a category.

The 1991 Gulf War under President George H. W. Bush was never formally concluded. Saddam Hussein, the dictatorial and dangerous president of Iraq, remained in control. In 1998, President Bill Clinton signed the Iraq Liberation Act, a policy that supported regime change but did not authorize the use of force. Plans for an invasion of Iraq were drawn up after the inauguration of President George W. Bush but were not put into action until 2002, following the al-Qaeda attacks of September 11, 2001, and the congressional Iraq War Resolution. A variety of factors were cited, including noncompliance with weapons inspections and the "capability and willingness to use weapons of mass destruction" (WMDs).

The rationale for Hussein's removal, however, became a moving target after it was determined that Iraq had no connection to al-Qaeda and no WMDs were found in the country. Attention shifted to more personal and less strategic issues. Iraq was a fixed target and much easier to strike than the amorphous al-Qaeda. It showed the public that the government was doing "something." And then there was the issue of the president's unfinished business. The news media began to revisit some comments the president made that sounded a bit like revenge. "No one envisioned him still standing. It's time to finish the task," he told the BBC in 1999.[17]

And, more famously, just before the invasion the president said, "After all, this is the guy that tried to kill my dad at one time," referring to an alleged assassination attempt on his father while he was visiting Kuwait in 1993.[18]

It was not divine intervention or a predestined choice that drove the United States into Iraq. It was a decision complicated by both fact and fiction. It came down to human judgment.

This is the key to how we will be remembered. A legacy starts with good intentions and ends with the weight of the correct judgments balanced against the wrong. The combination of personal credibility and demonstrated capability over time helps to explain why people trust their leaders. Arthur, as flawed as he was, exceeded the threshold required for trusted leadership.

But few will ever construct a ledger and list their accomplishments and failures, or those of another individual. Legacies are more than the facts and figures. The chances are that no one will remember every detail of what you did or didn't do, or exactly what you did or didn't say. But we do know how we feel about a person. That's what we're left with: an emotional memory. How we're remembered is our legacy.

CAMELOT WISDOM:

- Arthur's destiny was to be king, but his legacy was his own making. He wasn't aiming for a legacy; he was aiming for results.
- Ego helps to drive a preoccupation with executive image. Basing decisions on what will look the least bad, shifting with the latest polls or political winds, or driving for short-term results does not a legacy make.
- Although legacies can be whitewashed and altered, the honest and credible will not write the text of their own legacy. Lancelot learned that he should allow others to judge his deeds.
- Learning from history is vital, but the future can't be built if we're looking backward too frequently.
- Legacies are more than facts and figures; the quality of the work you produced, the fairness by which you led, and the strength of the relationships you forged are all part of the equation. More important, though, are the feelings you leave behind: it's how you're remembered that counts the most.

Yea, he who is a true king of men, will not say to himself, "Lo! I am worthy to be crowned with laurels;" but rather he will say to himself, "What more is there that I may do to make the world the better because of my endeavors?"[19]

CHAPTER 15

FINAL THOUGHTS: THE CAMELOT WISDOM TOP 10

Arthur led an unexpected life, one that he felt obligated to embrace out of duty and out of his own drive to right the wrongs of his day. Despite the passage of the centuries, he faced many of the same obstacles and disappointments, and reaped many of the same glories, that are with us today.

He was a hero and a coward. He was a visionary but also blind. Yet, he is remembered well and often. He was filled with good intentions and was able to follow through on some but not all of them. On balance, Arthur remains a great leader and a hero.

Arthur had no plan to leave behind a legacy or a checklist of critical success factors. He lived and led based on the lessons of his upbringing, those brought into view by his mentor, and his own interactions and experiences. Let's take one last moment to review the most relevant leadership attributes and behaviors that Arthur might have penned had he the time to reflect on his extraordinary life.

1. **Get help**. Never be afraid to seek advice or ask a question. Find a mentor or, at least, study the actions of others. The learning process must never stop.
2. **Exercise empathy**. Being aware of the feelings of others is not a weakness; it's a competitive strength. It enables you to form connections with staff and allies, and it allows for a greater understanding of competitors and adversaries.
3. **Remain ethical**. It's understood that ethics and fairness may be contextual, but they must be adhered to consistently, regardless of the situation. Competitive or legal issues may restrict the amount of your openness, but honesty knows no such limits.
4. **Confront issues**. We must move past anticipation and anxiety to address problems (and opportunities) in a timely way. Conflict shouldn't be sought to prove a point, but swift and thoughtful action is essential to set things on the best path.

5. **Draw boundaries**. We have a professional and a personal life. They may blend into each other, and we may draw our personal identity from our professional pursuits, but we must keep our perspective. Gather strength from both realms; we cannot live and work in a bubble or a vacuum.

6. **Plan ahead**. Virtually everything requires a plan, whether it's business development, issues or crisis preparedness, or staffing and succession. We need time to think. We need to know what our objectives are, what outcomes we seek, and how we intend to accomplish what we set out to do. We need to know how and when to slow down, speed up, stop, or restart. And we need research and information to track our progress and prepare for the unexpected.

7. **Involve others**. Identify and nurture the talent of others to expand your own reach and capabilities. The people you bring to the table, collectively or individually, need roundedness—a diversity of talents, experiences, and perspectives. Allow everyone to share in success if it is deserved. And continually expand your base of support through networking and relationship building.

8. **Use symbols**. People, objects, events, or even phrases can all become rallying points, icons for a common purpose. It's human nature to want to feel part of something larger, to belong, to associate with something that has a certain cachet. Facts are essential, but they may not be believed or embraced without a particular figure or image. Facts are most powerful when linked to persuasive language and proper tone and emotion.

9. **Create balance**. Think and feel. Analyze and do. Take in the perspective from 30,000 feet and down in the trenches. Apply yourself at work and at home. Rarely do we see or accomplish all or nothing; incrementalism may not seem satisfying, but it's the way most things operate and succeed. It may not be a straight and smooth road, but making progress, leaving improvements behind, is what's important.

10. **Understand control**. We may not like it, but there are matters we can influence and others we cannot; know the difference between the two. Aim for what's right, not expedient. Strive for outcomes, not for personal positioning. Define expectations and assign roles and responsibilities for yourself and for others to enhance accountability and results. What we have accomplished and how we have behaved determine how we'll be remembered—our legacy.

NOTES

INTRODUCTION

1. From *The Once and Future King* by T. H. White, copyright 1938, 1939, 1940, 1958, and renewed. Used by permission of G.P. Putnam's Sons, a division of Penguin Group (USA), Inc., Ace Edition (1987), p. 539.

CHAPTER 1

1. White, *The Once and Future King*, p. 34.
2. White, *The Once and Future King*, p. 11.
3. White, *The Once and Future King*, pp. 73, 74.
4. White, *The Once and Future King*, p. 121.
5. White, *The Once and Future King*, p. 183.
6. White, *The Once and Future King*, p. 46.
7. White, *The Once and Future King*, p. 223.
8. White, *The Once and Future King*, p. 554.
9. White, *The Once and Future King*, p. 106.
10. White, *The Once and Future King*, p. 377.
11. H. Pyle, *The Story of King Arthur and His Knights* (New York: Charles Scribner's and Sons, 1915), p. 178.
12. Pyle, *The Story of King Arthur and His Knights*, p. 87.
13. http://www.mentors.ca/mentorpairs.html.
14. http://www.merlinmentors.org.
15. White, *The Once and Future King*, p. 75.

CHAPTER 2

1. White, *The Once and Future King*, p. 332.
2. White, *The Once and Future King*, p. 90.
3. E. O'Brien, C. Hsing, and S. Konrath, Association for Psychological Science annual meeting, May 2010. "Changes in Dispositional Empathy Over Time in American College Students: A Meta-Analysis." Boston, MA.

4. Same as 3 above.

5. J. S. Lublin, "Top Brass Try Life in the Trenches," *The Wall Street Journal*, June 25, 2007.

6. White, *The Once and Future King*, p. 89.

7. White, *The Once and Future King*, p. 46.

8. White, *The Once and Future King*, p. 179.

9. White, *The Once and Future King*, p. 14.

10. R. Dunbar, *Grooming, Gossip, and the Evolution of Language* (Cambridge, MA: Harvard University Press, 1996), p. 35.

11. White, *The Once and Future King*, pp. 204, 205.

12. White, *The Once and Future King*, pp. 223, 225.

13. White, *The Once and Future King*, p. 485.

CHAPTER 3

1. White, *The Once and Future King*, p. 225.

2. P. F. Drucker, *Management: Tasks, Responsibilities, Practices* (New York: HarperBusiness, 1973), p. 128.

3. White, *The Once and Future King*, p. 247.

4. White, *The Once and Future King*, p. 364.

5. S. Case, "It's Time to Take It Apart; My Case for Dividing the Media Giant," *The Washington Post*, December 11, 2005.

6. D. Harding and Ted Rouse, "Human Due Diligence," *The Wall Street Journal*, October 2, 2007.

7. White, *The Once and Future King*, p. 52.

8. T. Malory, *Le Morte d'Arthur* (1469; New York: The Modern Library, 1999), pp. 10, 12.

9. White, *The Once and Future King*, p. 207.

10. White, *The Once and Future King*, p. 225.

11. White, *The Once and Future King*, pp. 231, 233.

12. J. Immelt, "Things Leaders Do," *Fast Company*, April 1, 2004, http://www.fastcompany.com/magazine/81/immelt.html.

13. White, *The Once and Future King*, pp. 246, 248.

14. H. W. Tesoriero et al., "Merck Loss Jolts Drug Giant, Industry," *The Wall Street Journal*, August 22, 2005.

15. Malory, *Le Morte d'Arthur*, pp. 100, 101.

16. White, *The Once and Future King*, p. 248.

17. White, *The Once and Future King*, p. 265.

18. White, *The Once and Future King*, p. 248.

CHAPTER 4

1. P. Oestreicher, "Knowledge Base: Perspectives on the State of Research Readiness in Public Relations," *Tactics*, March 2009, p. 13.

2. White, *The Once and Future King*, pp. 482, 509.

3. White, *The Once and Future King*, p. 550.

4. Malory, *Le Morte d'Arthur*, p. 46.

5. White, *The Once and Future King*, pp. 482, 509, 550.

6. White, *The Once and Future King*, pp. 87, 88.

CHAPTER 5

1. Malory, *Le Morte d'Arthur*, p. 691.

2. White, *The Once and Future King*, pp. 264, 265, 326.

3. Dunbar, *Grooming, Gossip, and the Evolution of Language*, p. 77.

4. Interview at online.wsj.com/video-center, April 16, 2010.

5. Malory, *Le Morte d'Arthur*, p. 1086.

6. Pyle, *The Story of King Arthur and His Knights*, p. 157.

7. Pyle, *The Story of King Arthur and His Knights*, p. 11.

8. Malory, *Le Morte d'Arthur*, p. 844.

9. J. Surowiecki, *The Wisdom of Crowds* (New York: Anchor Books, 2004), p. 176.

10. White, *The Once and Future King*, p. 331.

11. Malory, *Le Morte d'Arthur*, pp. 100, 101.

12. White, *The Once and Future King*, p. 427.

CHAPTER 6

1. White, *The Once and Future King*, pp. 319, 321.

2. White, *The Once and Future King*, p. 323.

3. White, *The Once and Future King*, p. 512.

4. I. Berlin, *The Hedgehog and the Fox: An Essay on Tolstoy's View of History* (New York: Simon and Schuster, 1953).

5. White, *The Once and Future King*, p. 183.

6. White, *The Once and Future King*, p. 74.

7. White, *The Once and Future King*, p. 567.

8. Malory, *Le Morte d'Arthur*, p. 347.

9. Malory, *Le Morte d'Arthur*, p. 835.

10. White, *The Once and Future King*, pp. 114, 115.

11. White, *The Once and Future King*, p. 464.

CHAPTER 7

1. White, *The Once and Future King*, p. 365.

2. White, *The Once and Future King*, p. 519.

3. White, *The Once and Future King*, p. 365.

4. White, *The Once and Future King*, p. 433.

5. White, *The Once and Future King*, p. 428.

6. White, *The Once and Future King*, pp. 432, 433.

7. White, *The Once and Future King*, p. 629.

8. White, *The Once and Future King*, p. 120.

CHAPTER 8

1. Malory, *Le Morte d'Arthur*, p. 407.

2. Malory, *Le Morte d'Arthur*, p. 416.

3. White, *The Once and Future King*, p. 57.

4. P. Sonne, "Hayward Fell Short of Modern CEO Demands," *The Wall Street Journal*, July 26, 2010.

5. White, *The Once and Future King*, p. 33.

6. White, *The Once and Future King*, p. 40.

7. Pyle, *The Story of King Arthur and His Knights*, p. 30.

8. Malory, *Le Morte d'Arthur*, p. 31.

9. Malory, *Le Morte d'Arthur*, p. 373.

10. Malory, *Le Morte d'Arthur*, p. 406.

11. White, *The Once and Future King*, p. 480.

12. White, *The Once and Future King*, pp. 562, 563.

CHAPTER 9

1. White, *The Once and Future King*, p. 621.

2. White, *The Once and Future King*, p. 298.

3. White, *The Once and Future King*, p. 244.

4. White, *The Once and Future King*, p. 522.

5. Malory, *Le Morte d'Arthur*, pp. 913, 914.

6. Malory, *The Once and Future King*, p. 355.

7. S. Lewandowsky et al., "Memory for Fact, Fiction, and Misinformation," *Psychological Science* 16:3 (2005): 190–195.

8. Malory, *Le Morte d'Arthur*, p. 483.

9. E. Bernstein, "The Dark Side of 'Webribution,'" *The Wall Street Journal*, December 3, 2009.

10. S. Hinduja and J. W. Patchin, *Bullying beyond the Schoolyard: Preventing and Responding to Cyberbullying* (Thousand Oaks, CA: Corwin Press, 2009).

11. http://googleblog.blogspot.com/2008/07/we-knew-web-was-big.html.

12. National Science Foundation, Division of Science Resources Statistics, Survey of Public Attitudes Toward and Understanding of Science and Technology, 1985–2001.

CHAPTER 10

1. White, *The Once and Future King*, p. 389.

2. A. P. Grammatikos, "The Genetic and Environmental Basis of Atopic Diseases," *Annals of Medicine* 40:7 (2008): 482–495.

3. Malory, *Le Morte d'Arthur*, p. 593.

4. White, *The Once and Future King*, p. 443.

5. T. H. White, *The Book of Merlyn* (Austin, TX: University of Texas Press, 1977), p. 5.

6. H. Pyle, *The Story of the Champions of the Round Table* (New York: Charles Scribner's Sons, 1905), p. 45.

7. White, *The Once and Future King*, p. 579.

8. White, *The Once and Future King*, p. 432.

9. Malory, *Le Morte d'Arthur*, p. 919.

10. White, *The Once and Future King*, p. 579.

11. White, *The Once and Future King*, p. 631.

CHAPTER 11

1. White, *The Once and Future King*, p. 266.

2. P. Oestreicher, "A Pioneer Passes," http://c-o-i-n-s.blogspot.com/2009/01/pioneer-passes.html.

3. Malory, *Le Morte d'Arthur*, pp. 31, 32.

4. A. Levitt, "The Imperial CEO Is No More," *The Wall Street Journal*, March 17, 2005.

5. Gary Weiss, "What 'Advice' Will Artie Levitt Give Goldman Sachs?" http://garyweiss.blogspot.com/2009/06/what-advice-will-artie-levitt-give.html.

6. White, *The Once and Future King*, pp. 421, 550.

7. White, *The Once and Future King*, p. 245.

CHAPTER 12

1. White, *The Once and Future King*, p. 222.

2. White, *The Once and Future King*, p. 222.

3. White, *The Once and Future King*, p. 630.

4. P. F. Drucker, *The Effective Executive* (New York: HarperBusiness, 1966), p. 157.

5. R. E. Jung et al., "Biochemical Support for the 'Threshold' Theory of Creativity: A Magnetic Resonance Spectroscopy Study," *Journal of Neuroscience* 29:16 (2009): 5319–5325.

6. R. E. Jung et al., "Neuroanatomy of Creativity, Human Brain Mapping," *Journal of Neuroscience* 31:3 (2010): 398–409.

7. C. von Clausewitz, *On War* (1832, translation by M. Howard and P. Paret, Princeton: Princeton University Press, 1989).

8. White, *The Once and Future King*, p. 552.

9. White, *The Once and Future King*, pp. 79, 80.

10. White, *The Once and Future King*, p. 143.

11. White, *The Once and Future King*, p. 107.

12. White, *The Once and Future King*, pp. 122, 124, 128.

13. White, *The Book of Merlyn*, p. 11.

14. 2010 IBM Global CEO Study, http://www.ibm.com/ceostudy.

15. Attributed to Kyung-Hee Kim in P. Bronson and A. Merryman, "The Creativity Crisis," *Newsweek,* July 19, 2010.

16. White, *The Book of Merlyn*, p. 11.

CHAPTER 13

1. 2010 National Association of Corporate Directors Public Company Governance Survey.

2. National Association of Corporate Directors, "Strategic Planning and CEO Succession Top List of Director Concerns for 3rd Year in a Row" (October 15, 2007).

3. White, *The Once and Future King*, pp. 636, 637.

4. Malory, *Le Morte d'Arthur*, p. 924.

5. Pyle, *The Story of King Arthur and His Knights*, p. 301.

6. Malory, *Le Morte d'Arthur*, p. 932.

7. Pyle, *The Story of King Arthur and His Knights*, p. 2.

8. S. Leonard and W. Reiss, *Stew Leonard, My Story* (Colle & Company, 2009).

9. Attributed to Akio Toyoda in N. Shirouzu, "Inside Toyota, Executives Trade Blame over Debacle," *The Wall Street Journal,* April 14, 2010.

10. Shirouzu, "Inside Toyota."

11. Reported in A. Vance and M. Richtel, "Hewlett Took a P.R. Firm's Advice in the Hurd Case," *The New York Times,* August, 9, 2010.

12. J. Reingold, "The $79 Billion Handoff," *Fortune,* December 7, 2009.

13. Reingold, "The $79 Billion Handoff."

14. White, *The Once and Future King*, p. 219.

15. J. Welch and J. A. Byrne, *Jack: Straight from the Gut* (New York: Warner Books, 2003), p. 426.

CHAPTER 14

1. White, *The Once and Future King*, p. 180.

2. Pyle, *The Story of King Arthur and His Knights*, p. 25.

3. W. Shakespeare, *Twelfth Night* (1602), Act II, Scene V.

4. White, *The Once and Future King*, p. 617.

5. White, *The Once and Future King*, p. 628.

6. C. Liu and D. Yermack, "Where Are the Shareholders' Mansions? CEOs' Home Purchases, Stock Sales, and Subsequent Company Performance," Social Science Research Network, October 17, 2007, http://ssrn.com/abstract=970413.

7. Pyle, *The Story of King Arthur and His Knights*, p. 312.

8. Pyle, *The Story of King Arthur and His Knights*, pp. 74, 75.

9. Pyle, *The Story of King Arthur and His Knights*, p. 75.

10. Pyle, *The Story of the Champions of the Round Table*, p. 45.

11. White, *The Once and Future King*, p. 630.

12. "Microsoft Jumps to No. 1 in National Corporate Reputation Survey, Harris Interactive" (February 1, 2007), http://www.harrisinteractive.com/NEWS/allnewsbydate.asp?NewsID=1170.

13. "Berkshire Hathaway Ranks #1 on Corporate Reputation, according to 11th Annual Harris Interactive U.S. Reputation Quotient® (RQ®) Survey," April 5, 2010, http://www.harrisinteractive.com/vault/Harris_Interactive_News_2010_04_05.pdf.

14. M. O'Keefe, *New York Daily News*, July 13, 2010, http://www.nydaily news.com/sports/baseball/yankees/2010/07/13/2010-07-13_howie_spira_hired_by_george_steinbrenner_to_help_smear_dave_winfield_still_holds.html.

15. White, *The Once and Future King*, p. 521.

16. White, *The Once and Future King*, p. 631.

17. Reported in P. Baker, "Hussein and the Bushes: Conflicts Shaped Two Presidencies," *The Washington Post*, December 31, 2006, http://www.washington-post.com/wp-dyn/content/article/2006/12/30/AR2006123000663.html.

18. http://www.youtube.com/watch?v=OC5dfneoHcE.

19. Pyle, *The Story of King Arthur and His Knights*, p. 98.

INDEX

accomplishment, 59–63, 90, 92, 106,
    135. *See also* leadership; promotion
accountability, 35, 43
accumulated wisdom. *See*
    conventional wisdom
acquisition, 24–25
advice, 5
Agravaine, xviii, 13, 66, 77, 81,
    85–87, 124
ambassadors, 39
AMF (formerly American Machine
    and Foundry), 25
ancient wisdom, xiii. *See also*
    Camelot wisdom
anger, 66, 77
animal-world adventures, 13,
    15–17, 59
AOL (America Online), 25
Apple, 57
Art of War, The (Sun Tzu), 21
Arthur, King, 23, 81–82, 106; advice
    and, 5–6; animal-world adven-
    tures of, 13, 15–17, 59; battle
    and, 20–21, 77–78, 83–85,
    97–98, 113, 117, 130–131;
    change implementation and,
    35, 36, 37, 38–40; equal justice
    and, xvi, 38–39, 40–41; evolu-
    tion of, xvii–xx, 27, 59–60, 92,
    127–129, 34; family politics

and, 51–52, 80–81, 85–86,
    98, 124; goals of, 65–66, 71;
    independent thought and,
    xv, 113–114; management
    and, 31–33, 47, 48, 101–102;
    philosophy of, 26, 27, 31, 61,
    109; and the status quo, 17–18;
    succession and, 119–121; unifi-
    cation of England and, 28–29.
    See also Equal Justice; Merlin;
    Might for Right
Arthur Andersen, 80, 117
articulation, 50
Aurelius, Marcus, xiii
avoidance, 78–79
awareness, 77
balance, 91–93, 96, 98, 100
banishment, xviii

Bank of America, 123
battle, 73, 85; of Bedegraine, xix,
    77–78, 84; business, 75, 90;
    disappointment and, 117,
    130–131; tactics, 83–84;
    wisdom of, 20–21, 113
battle-picking, 73, 76, 78, 83
Bedivere, Sir, 120
Berlin, Isaiah, 58
big idea, 69, 70
Boo.com, 79

About the Author

PAUL OESTREICHER started his career as a scientist. After an undergraduate degree in biology from the University of Rochester, and a PhD in nutritional sciences from Rutgers University, he completed a postdoctoral fellowship in pharmacology while with Wyeth Laboratories. He then went on to the clinical research and development department at Hoffmann-La Roche. Following his passion for health and science education, he moved into their public policy and communications department. He also had executive roles at Genaissance Pharmaceuticals, Edelman, and Hill & Knowlton, and established Oestreicher Communications, LLC.

Inspired by his children, Dr. Oestreicher shifted gears and founded TagsMania, LLC (www.tagsmania.com), where he designs and manufactures distinctive toys and gifts. He is also an adjunct professor at New York University's School of Continuing and Professional Studies, Division of Programs in Business, advising graduate students and teaching courses on research process and methodology and strategic communication.

He is the father of four daughters and lives with his wife, a nurse educator and psychoanalytic psychotherapist, in Connecticut.